Believers

Worship in a Multi-Faith Community

Celia Collinson and Campbell Miller

Photographs by Nick Hedges and David Richardson

CLHBEL

Hodder & Stoughton

LONDON SYDNEY AUCKLAND TORONTO

© 1981 Celia Collinson and Campbell Miller

First published in Great Britain 1981
Eighth impression 1992

British Library Cataloguing in Publication Data
Collinson, Celia
  Believers
  1. Religion
  I. Title   II. Miller, Campbell
  200   BL48

ISBN 0 7131 0525 9

Typeset in VIP Century Schoolbook by Western Printing Services
Ltd, Bristol
Printed and bound in Great Britain for the educational
publishing division of Hodder and Stoughton Limited, Mill Road,
Dunton Green, Sevenoaks, Kent by The Bath Press, Avon

Preface

'I'm a Believer' was the title of an exhibition of photographs on display in Wolverhampton in 1976. The photographs, taken as a result of the efforts of the Wolverhampton Inter-Faith Group, showed people at worship in the various communities of faith in the area. The exhibition made a considerable impact on the community and, in particular, stimulated the interest of young people in local schools. This led to the development of the idea that the photographs could form the basis for useful work in Religious Education in school.

Worship is often a neglected aspect of the study of religion in the setting of school, perhaps because it is difficult to convey an atmosphere and a feeling for such religious experiences in words alone. The photographs have captured the feelings of the worshippers, and go a considerable way towards giving children the opportunity to gain insights into this important expression of religion.

Our aim is to introduce pupils to aspects of worship and to foster a sympathetic feeling for worship as it is practised in various faiths, within a multi-faith community in Britain today.

We have in mind, especially, pupils of lower-secondary age, though we have also found the material useful with some older groups such as those preparing for a C.S.E. examination.

There are, of course, many different expressions of worship even within each faith, especially in the case of Christianity and Hinduism. We do not feel that it is helpful to dwell on such differences with children of the age we have in mind, so our look at Christian worship, for example, does not dwell on different denominations, but rather looks across the spectrum of Christian worship.

We must emphasise that we are endeavouring to give a picture of worship *as we have found it* within the religious communities represented in the Wolverhampton area.

We hope that pupils will gain from this study a clearer insight into the variety of ways in which ordinary folk approach their god, and will have some appreciation of the richness of such religious experience.

Acknowledgements

The Authors wish to record their gratitude to the following:
members of the various religious communities in Wolverhampton for their willingness to talk and help them in their understanding of the different ways of worship;
Mrs Ivy Gutridge, the secretary of Wolverhampton Inter-Faith Group for her considerable help, especially her careful reading of the typescript and her valuable comments and suggestions;
the photographers, Nick Hedges and David Richardson for their willingness to assist in this use of their photographs;
Phil Coats for his efforts to meet their needs for drawings to supplement the photographs;
the Inspector and Staff of the Wolverhampton Education Authority Teaching Resources Centre for assistance with pilot schemes for the material;
the Resources Department of Colton Hills School, Wolverhampton for their advice and practical assistance;
Mr D. Parsons, Headmaster and Mr K Berry, Deputy Headmaster, of Colton Hills School for their encouragement.

The publishers would like to thank Nick Hedges for permission to reproduce all photographs except those on pp 10, 11, 12, 13, 17b, 18b, 19, 20l & r, 42, 44, 48l & r, 62, 79t which were taken by David Richardson; and the following:
Government of India Tourist Office, p 39; India Office Library, p 45t; Mansell Collection Ltd., p 51; The Bible Society, p 54.
The Publishers also wish to thank the following for permission to reproduce copyright material:
The American Bible Society for a passage from the Greek New Testament (Third Edition) published by the United Bible Societies © American Bible Society 1966, 1968, 1975; Eyre and Spottiswoode (Publishers) Ltd for an extract from the Authorized Version of the Bible, which is Crown Copyright, used by permission; National Council of the Churches of Christ in the U.S.A. for Psalm 137 from the Revised Standard Version Common Bible, copyrighted © 1973; Oxford and Cambridge University Presses for an extract from the New English Bible second edition © 1970 and the Singer's Prayer-Book Publication Committee for an extract from their Authorised Daily Prayer Book.

Contents

To the pupils of Colton Hills School,
Wolverhampton, past, present and future
and
to communities everywhere in the hope
of greater understanding.

Part I
Places of Worship

Introduction

Every religion has a special place set aside in the community which is for worship; a place where the followers of that faith can feel that they are close to their god.

Why do people find it necessary, or at least helpful, to have such a place for worship? Why not, for example, sit in a beautiful garden admiring the beauty of the world around us and offer worship to God in our own way? We find that the Christian has his church or chapel, the Jew has his synagogue, the Hindu has his temple, the Sikh has his gurdwara or temple and the Muslim has his mosque. All of these will have many differences but all will have a common use – they are all places of worship.

In answer to the question why do people of various religious faiths feel it important to have such centres for worship, the most obvious answer is that people who follow a particular faith want a suitable building where they can meet together conveniently. If they have such a place they can surround themselves with various objects which help them to worship and they can sometimes include certain features in the design of the building which remind them of God and other aspects of their faith.

Very often such places of worship become 'sacred places' to the worshippers and they would not like to see the building used for any other purpose than for worship; when they enter the building they treat it with great respect, for example by covering the head, or removing their shoes, or talking only in a whisper.

Before we explore some such places of worship and see what people do in them here is a task which will help to prepare you.

Task 1
In this introduction we have used the following words:
worship   church   chapel
temple   sacred.
Look up in a dictionary and write in your book what each means.

1

Hindu

Hinduism is the ancient faith which stems from India. There are a number of gods worshipped by the Hindu, but many would say that each of these gods is a part of the One God to whom the Hindu usually refers by the one word **Om** or **Aum**. Another way of expressing this is to say that the Hindu believes God is without form and that he is so great and so complex that no one idea of him is sufficient, so each Hindu god is yet another way of expressing an idea about one little part of the One God.

Vishnu

Vishnu is one of the important Hindu gods and Hindus believe that he has appeared in the world of men in various forms at various times. One of the ways in which it is believed he appeared is in the form of Rama, a prince who lived in north India. (You will find one of the stories about him in 'Sacred Writings in Worship' on page 42.)

Krishna

Another of the forms in which Hindus say Vishnu appeared is in the person of Krishna about whom there are many stories in the Mahabharata, one of the Hindu sacred writings. Many Hindus, in fact, refer to Krishna himself as a god and worship him especially.

The figure of Krishna often appears on the shrine which is a focal point in a Hindu temple.

One of the best known stories about Krishna tells of his birth. It tells of evil rulers who made life miserable for their subjects and who were thought to be demons disguised as men. Brahma, the creator god, sent good spirits to fight these evil forces and he also promised that soon, the god Vishnu would be born into the world.

There was a princess called Devaki, wife of Vasudeva. Devaki had an evil brother called Kansa, who believed that Devaki's eighth child would kill him. He intended to kill his sister to make sure she never had an eighth child, but Vasudeva managed to persuade him to spare her life.

Kansa still believed his own life would be threatened by Devaki's son, so he made sure that each time a son was born to his sister, the child was killed. Eventually he awaited the birth of an eighth child; meanwhile the god Vishnu appeared to Vasudeva and told him that he would enter the world in the form of Devaki's next son. Because Vishnu had appeared to him, it is said that Vasudeva began to shine like the sun and as Devaki prepared for the birth of her son, she too began to shine brightly as the moon. Kansa was deeply troubled when he saw his sister and her husband shining with this heavenly glory.

Krishna

Eventually the child was born and on that day, they say that all the stars shone more brightly than ever before and rivers which had been dry were flowing with clear water; forests seemed alive with the songs of birds and the humming of bees. Vasudeva bowed low before his new born son and said that he recognised him as Lord of the Universe. Devaki also bowed before her son saying, 'Truly, you are a god of heaven, the Lord Vishnu. You care for the whole world; you are the lamp which guides men through life.'

In order to protect the child whom they called Krishna, from the evil Kansa, Vasudeva took the child to the kingdom of Nanda, the cow-herd king. Quickly, with the help of the gods, he took the

Krishna and Radha as part of Hindu Shrine

baby girl just born to Nanda's wife, and left Krishna in its place. So Krishna was kept safe and was brought up in the simple home of Nanda and he mixed freely with ordinary country people who loved him and all recognised him as no ordinary child, but as the Lord of the whole world.

Krishna is usually shown playing a flute; this is because in one of the other well-known stories about him he played on a flute and persuaded a group of milk maids to leave their families and dance with him in the moonlight. This story was thought by Hindus to represent the fact that, while family relationships are important, to follow and to love the god is even more important. In the story, Krishna especially loved the milk maid, Radha, and many Hindus think Radha represents the soul of a person; as Krishna loved Radha, so the god loves the soul of each person. Radha usually appears beside Krishna on the shrine in a Hindu place of worship.

A Temple for Krishna

One of the Hindu temples in our community was called 'Shri Krishan Mandir' which means 'the Blessed Krishna Temple'; there the worship of god was specially directed towards Krishna. (Unfortunately, this temple, which was based in an old house, has since been demolished and the Hindu community are at present saving for a new purpose-built temple which they hope to erect on the same site as the old one.)

The shrine on this page was in this temple and formed the focal point for the worshippers.

Task 1
Look carefully at the photograph of Krishna and draw a picture of the god. Write a few paragraphs about Krishna

using the information you have been given. Perhaps you can add to this from any books you can borrow from the library.

Finding Out About the Temple

In a series of talks with the leaders of the temple we asked questions to discover as much as we could about how this group of Hindus offer worship:

Our question: We were asked to remove our shoes before entering your temple; why was this?

Answer: It is a custom among Hindus that we remove our shoes at the temple as a mark of respect, for we think of this as a holy place.

Our question: We notice, by the sweet smell as we entered, that incense is burned in the temple. Can you tell us why Hindus do this?

Answer: People who enter the temple often light these tapers or joss-sticks, which gives the temple the special odour; this incense also purifies the air and kills any germs and we believe that it is pleasing to the god.

Hindu worshippers facing the shrine

Our question: Can you tell us why you have a large shell on the table where the incense is burning?

Answer: The conch shell is used to call the people to worship. It is quite difficult to learn to blow it properly but it sounds similar to a horn when you have mastered the art. In India, you see, the conch would be blown in the temple and the villagers would hear it in their homes and know that it was time for worship. We also blow the conch at times of special rejoicing in the temple.

Our question: There are three bells on the table; do you ring these to show you are going to begin an act of worship?

Answer: Yes the ringing of the bells shows that prayer is about to begin.

Our question: May we know why you have a bowl of food in front of the shrine?

Answer: This food we call **prashad**. It is regarded as very sacred to us because the food has been offered to the gods by the worshippers. At the end of an act of worship it is then shared out between those present and some of it will often be taken to those who were unable to be present.

Our question: The figures on the shrine look very beautiful and well cared for; whose responsibility is it to care for them?

Answer: The statues are washed and dressed once a week in a private ceremony. This is also done whenever we are about to celebrate a special festival. This is usually done by a priest but since we do not have a priest, any man with a responsible position in the temple can do it. The clothing for the figures has been made by the ladies of our community.

Musicians in Hindu worship

Our question: We notice that music plays a part in your worship; what instruments do you use?

Answer: A **shimta** is used to give the rhythm. It is a long instrument with small cymbals attached to it. The musician plays by shaking the instrument. Two kinds of drums are used which we call **dohlki** and **tabla**. The third instrument you can see is a harmonium which the musician pumps with one hand and plays with the other.

Our question: Are children welcome to attend worship in your temple?

Answer: Yes, they certainly are; children and babies come with their parents: sometimes they even play an active part in the worship. The two little girls you see in the photograph occasionally lead the chanting of prayers. One of these girls is learning Sanskrit which is the ancient language in which some of our holy books are written.

Our question: This temple obviously is an old house which your community of Hindu worshippers has made into a place of worship; how does this compare with Hindu temples in your country of India?

Answer: In India, usually the temple would be a building specially designed and built for the purpose. Often it would have been a place of Hindu worship for centuries. It would not, of course, be possible for us to have such a temple in our town here, so we have to make do with this old house. In an Indian temple, of course, you would find a shrine similar to the one we have here and that, for us, is the most important feature of the temple.

Our question: Does every Hindu community living in Britain have a temple like this?

Answer: Oh no! Many would not be able to find a suitable building, or could not afford one. I could take you, however, to some homes of Hindu families, where there is a shrine in one of the rooms and

Children at worship

that has become their temple; sometimes it has also become the temple for their Hindu Friends and neighbours. There is such a temple not far from here in the home of Mr and Mrs Ratilal Patel.

13

The Home Temple

We visited this house to which we had been directed; it looked similar in every respect to the other houses in the road and when we entered we saw that every room in the house was just as you would expect, apart from a large room at the back on the ground floor. Before we entered this room we did as our host Mr Patel did, and removed our shoes because, although we were in a home, we were about to enter a place of worship. We could smell the same fragrance of incense which we had noticed at the other temple.

This room was indeed a temple in a house! How colourful it was! Along the wall where once had been the fireplace there was a central shrine and two

Hindus at worship in the Home Temple

The Home Temple

smaller shrines on each side of the chimney breast. There were pictures and photographs about Hinduism hung on the other three walls. The Patel family worship in this temple every evening, but on Thursday evenings they are joined by other Hindus in the community. As part of their worship Mr Patel plays a harmonium and everyone joins in hymns of praise. Sometimes the room is so crowded that some of the worshippers have to sit in the hall or even on the stairs.

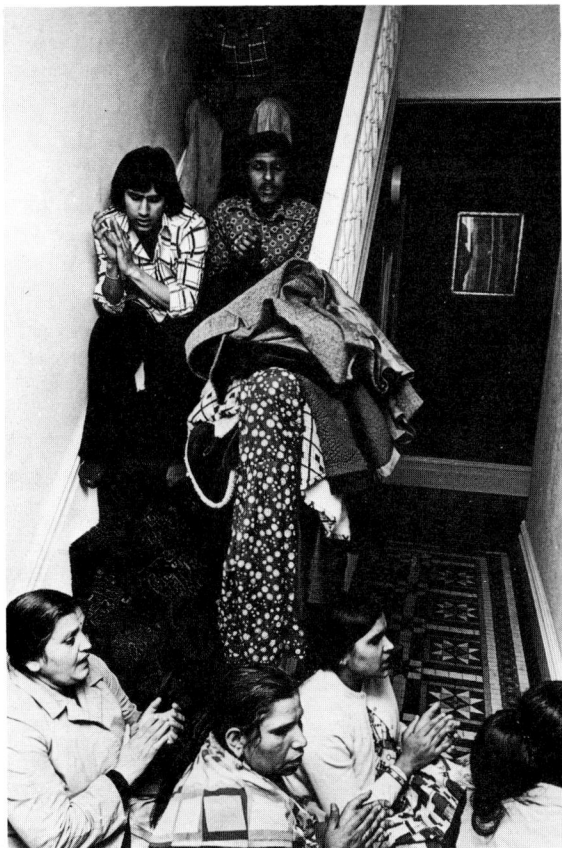

Task 2
In the photographs of the temple you can see the following: write a sentence about each of them to show their purpose in the temple: (a) bells, (b) joss-sticks, (c) prashad (include a list of the foods which you can see in the photograph opposite), (d) a shimta, (e) a conch shell.

Task 3
Using your knowledge of a Hindu temple, conduct an imaginary interview with Mr Patel in which you ask the following questions: (a) why are there no chairs for the worshippers in the temple? (b) what similarities are there between this home temple and the other Hindu temple in the community? (c) why are there so many pictures of gods and goddesses in the temple?

Task 4
Study the photograph of the home temple carefully; make a list of any items which you are able to recognise in it and briefly say what you think the use of each would be in the temple.

Task 5
Write a few paragraphs in which you give answers to the following questions: (a) how would your parents re-act to the suggestion that a room in your house should be used exclusively as a place of worship? (b) why do some Hindus living in this country do this? (c) what do you see as the advantages and the disadvantages of this? (d) what does having such a temple in the home say about the people's attitude to their religion?

2
Jewish

The faith followed by a Jew is usually referred to as Judaism. The origins of Judaism go back about five thousand years to Abraham, about whom we read in Genesis, the first book of what Christians call 'the Old Testament'. Abraham is sometimes referred to as 'the Father of the Jewish people', in the sense that they regard him as their first ancestor. The other great character from the past whom Jews regard as having given considerable form and content to their faith, is Moses who lived over three thousand years ago.

Many Jews live today in their traditional home land, which is now called the State of Israel, but large numbers of Jews are to be found in almost every country of the world and wherever there is a community of Jews almost certainly you will find a synagogue where they worship.

How Synagogues Began

Many centuries ago the main place of worship for Jews was a temple in Jerusalem. When their land, then known as Judah, was invaded by the Babylonians and the city of Jerusalem itself was captured and destroyed in 587 BC, many of the Jewish people were carried off captive to Babylon. There, many of them wanted to keep their faith alive and so they began to meet for worship, at first in the open-air, then

later they probably erected small buildings in which they could meet.

When about 538 BC Cyrus, king of Persia conquered the Babylonians, he allowed the Jews to return to their home in Judah. There, the practice began in Babylon, was continued, and gradually, little meeting houses sprang up in each community for worship.

Today you can find such Jewish places of worship called **synagogues** all over the world, wherever there is a community of Jewish people. The word 'synagogue' stems from a Greek word which means 'a gathering', i.e. a gathering of people; the name however is given to the building in which they gather for their worship.

Finding Out About A Local Synagogue

The synagogue in our community is a small one for there are not very many

Jews in this community. It is laid down among Jews that before a synagogue service of worship can take place, there must be at least ten men present. Quite often, for this reason and because they like sometimes to worship in a larger community, they travel to the nearby city where many more Jews live and they join them in worship in their synagogue, which you can see from the photographs on this page, is very much larger. Look carefully at the above photograph; can you spot anything which tells you it is a Jewish place of worship?

Although this is a much grander and more spacious building, its layout of important features is basically the same as a synagogue anywhere else.

Plan of a synagogue

We asked the **Rabbi** (i.e. the Minister), Dr Brooks, whom you see holding a scroll from which the scriptures are read, some questions about this Jewish place of worship:

Our question: Dr Brooks, we notice that you are wearing a little cap on your head; will you explain why you keep this on when you are in the synagogue?

Answer: The little cap is called a **yarmulke** and men always wear this when at worship; indeed many Jewish men wear it all the time because they regard all of life as an act of worship and say that always they are under God's heaven. Some Jews say it is worn in synagogue as a mark of reverence for the place of worship.

Our question: We notice there is a gallery in the synagogue; do people sit up there in normal services of worship?

Answer: The tradition in a Jewish synagogue is that the men sit downstairs and the ladies sit upstairs in the gallery. During the war, the ladies of our synagogue were worried about being upstairs in case of a bombing raid, so they were allowed to sit downstairs and this has continued. In a normal service you would find that the centre block of pews is occupied by the ladies and the men are sitting in the pews at either side. At special festival times when more worshippers are here, the ladies return to sitting in the gallery.

Our question: Most of the seats have names on them; what do these mean?

Answer: When a Jew becomes a member of the local synagogue, he pays rent for a seat and his name is then put on that seat. Sometimes you will see more than one name on a seat; that is because when a man dies, quite often his son will take over his seat and leave his fathers name on it, adding his own name.

The Rabbi

Our question: This practice of paying rent for a seat in the synagogue seems rather strange; what is the reason for it?

Answer: The reason is that there is no collection taken in the synagogue, because a strict Jew is not supposed to carry any money on the Sabbath day, the special weekly holy day for the Jews, so these seat rents represent the income of the synagogue, to pay for the up-keep of the building, the salary of the Rabbi, etc.

Our question: Do all seats cost the same?

Answer: No! The rent for seats near the door is 25p per week, and the rent is more, the nearer you are to the **Bimah** (see pp 46 and 49). Those nearest the front are 75p per week.

Our question: We are looking now at what must be the focal point of the synagogue, behind the Bimah. Can you tell us about what we see there?

Answer: You are looking at the Ark, which is where the sacred scrolls of the scriptures are kept. The curtain over the Ark is open just now and you can see the scrolls inside.

Our question: What about the beautiful window above the Ark with the strange writing on it?

Answer: The strange writing is, of course, Hebrew, the language of our religion and the ancient language of the Jewish people. The design of the window represents the two tablets of stone given to Moses, our great leader from centuries ago, containing ten commandments. These are in this position in the synagogue so that every worshipper is reminded of the importance of God's law.

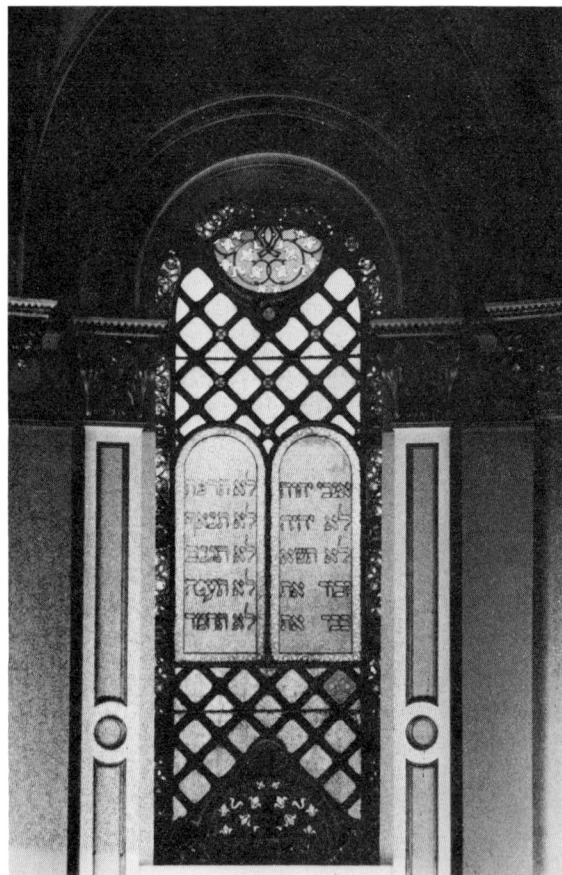

Our question: What is the significance of the crown which we see above the Ark?

Answer: The crown you see above the Ark is a reminder that the Torah is a crown for the Jewish people. The Torah is the law contained in the first five books of the Bible. Jews try to live by the teaching of these five books of Moses above everything else. To the right of the Ark you can see the Hebrew letter which represents a K; this stands for Keter which means crown and to the left is the letter T which stands for Torah which means the law. This is our constant reminder that the Jewish law is above everything else for us.

Our question: Also above the Ark we see what looks like an 'Aladdin's Lamp'; What is its purpose?

Answer: Every synagogue, whether in Israel or in Birmingham has such a light above the Ark, although its shape may be different and the light may be made by electricity, as here, or by gas, oil or candle. The lamp is called in Hebrew **Ner Tamid**, which means, 'everlasting light'. This custom is traced back to the fact that a lamp always burned in the Jewish Temple centuries ago. It is a reminder to us that God is always present in the synagogue and from here can shine out the light of the Torah. Our light is wired up so that even if I turned out every other light in the synagogue, this one would stay alight.

Task 1
Imagine you are describing a synagogue for someone who has not even seen a photograph of one; study the photographs in this section carefully and write your description using the information in this section to help you.

Task 2
Make a list of key words connected with a synagogue and write a brief note about each one: begin with *synagogue* itself: other examples are: *Rabbi, yarmulke.*

Task 3
You will find the Ten Commandments in your Bible in Exodus: chapter 20, verses 2–17: obviously the Hebrew words on the window in the synagogue are a shortened version of each commandment; write in your book a short version of each one.

Task 4
If there is a synagogue near where you live, ask your teacher to arrange a visit. Make a list of questions you would like to ask about the synagogue and the worship which takes place there.

3
Christian

There are many different kinds of Christian places of worship, for the Christian faith has been expressed in many different ways: some Christians are known as Roman Catholics, some as Anglicans or Church of England, others as Methodists, others as Baptists, others again as Presbyterians and some as the Society of Friends, to mention only a few. Their places of worship might be different but they have in common their faith in Jesus Christ, the founder of Christianity.

Christians usually call their place of worship **church**, though it would be more accurate, perhaps to call it 'the place where the church meets', for the word church really means the people and not the building.

Here are pictures of the outside of two Christian churches.

Task 1

(a) Study these pictures carefully and write a description of one of them.

(b) Imagine you are looking down on to the building from the air. Draw the shape you would see and write a short paragraph saying why you think that shape is used in the design of many Christian churches.

(c) Find out the name which is given to the tall tapering structure which you see on the roof in one picture. (Notice that the other one also has little structures like this on top of the tower.) What significance might this have to the people who worship?

Inside a Church

Imagine you have looked around the outside of these churches and now we are taking you inside. We are entering as quietly as we can because worship has already begun. Let us stand at the back and discover what is going on and what there is of importance in this building. Surely this is the best time to find out about the inside of a place of worship – when people are actually using it!

Task 2

Study the picture and the diagram carefully. Imagine you are standing at the back: describe what you see in front of you and try to include some description of what is going on in the worship.

Praying

You will have noticed that in the photograph on the left the people are sitting on the pews. In many churches, though by no means all of them, there is something in front of each pew on which the worshippers can kneel for prayers.

We have moved into a different church building and are looking from the front and find the congregation, (or most of them!) offering prayers. You will be looking more closely later on at how important this is in Christian worship.

Singing

You are now going to visit briefly different places of Christian worship. Although each building is clearly very different from the other and the people are dressed differently, there can be no doubt that music is the one activity which they have in common. A Christian church is usually a place where people, at some point in their worship, sing! (If you look back to the photograph on the left perhaps you can spot something there which tells you that they sing in that church also?) Sometimes the worshipper feels very inspired by the words and the tune of the hymn which is being sung.

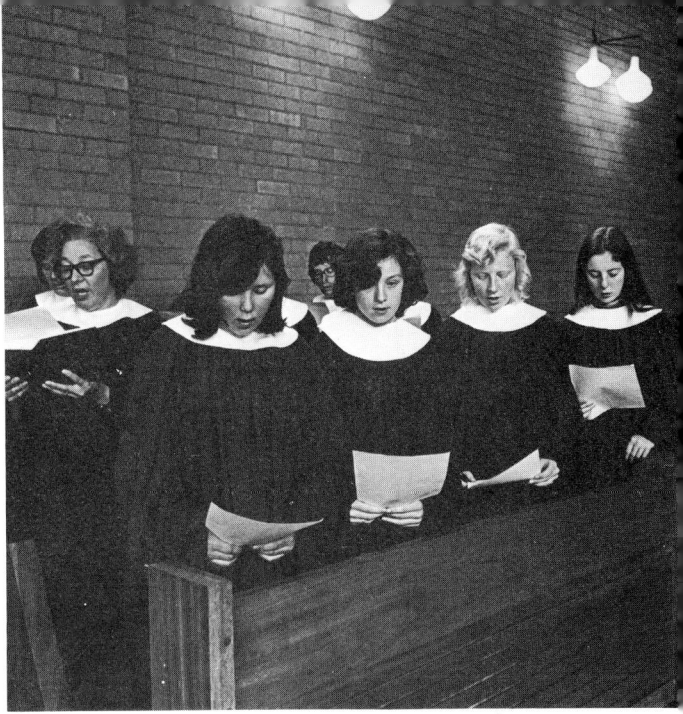

Task 3

(a) Here are verses from the last of the Psalms – Psalm 150, verses 3 to 6:

'Praise him with trumpet sound;
Praise him with lute and harp!
Praise him with timbrel and dance;
Praise him with strings and pipe!
Praise him with sounding cymbals;
Praise him with loud clashing cymbals!
Let everything that breathes praise the Lord!
Praise the Lord!'

Imagine these as instructions given to worshippers many centuries ago. Try to write some lines which would be suitable instructions about praising God for the worshippers in these last five photographs.

(b) Try to make up a hymn which you can imagine some of these worshippers singing. Remember a hymn is really a poem about some religious theme, for example, giving thanks to God, praising him for nature, etc. If you can make your words fit a hymn tune you already know, perhaps you can have your hymn sung in school assembly!

The Sermon

The pulpit

Most Christian churches have a pulpit. It may be of stone and decorated by many carvings. (You can see another one like this if you look at the photograph on page 24.) It may however be of wood and rather more plain. In some churches the whole service is conducted from the pulpit, but in others, only the sermon is preached from there.

The sermon is an address or speech given by the Priest or Minister in which, usually, he takes a verse from the Bible and talks about it. His aim is perhaps to inspire his congregation, or to challenge them to some action, or to help them understand better some aspect of their faith.

Task 4

(a) Write a paragraph in your book about the pulpit and what it is used for.

(b) Imagine that the sermon was based on the following verse from the Bible; 'This command comes to us from Christ himself: that he who loves God must also love his brother [i.e. other people]'. (1 John: chapter 4, verse 21). Write down briefly some of the things the preacher might have said about the idea expressed in that verse.

The Blessing

Usually the final act of worship in a Christian church is when the Priest or Minister says a closing prayer or blessing which is often called 'the Benediction'. Usually the worshippers stand for this.

The words of the Benediction vary: the commonest one is: 'The grace of the Lord Jesus Christ, and the love of God, and

the fellowship of the Holy Spirit, be with you all, Amen'.

Another example is:

'Unto God's gracious mercy and protection we commit you. And the blessing of God Almighty, the Father, the Son and the Holy Spirit, be upon you and remain with you for ever, Amen.'

Perhaps the blessing is a reminder that Christians should see the time they spend in their place of worship not so much as the most important part of their day, but a way in which they find help to cope with all the other experiences of life in the world outside. The blessing then, is a kind of prayer asking for God to go with them back into every day life.

While the majority of worshippers make their way out of church, back to their various other activities, sometimes, in some churches, there are those who linger a little longer and pray a little more.

Task 5

As a class project, find out the various Christian places of worship in your district. Divide into groups, each group responsible for one place of worship. You could interview the Priest, Minister or leader and gather information about how he and his people regard their place of worship.

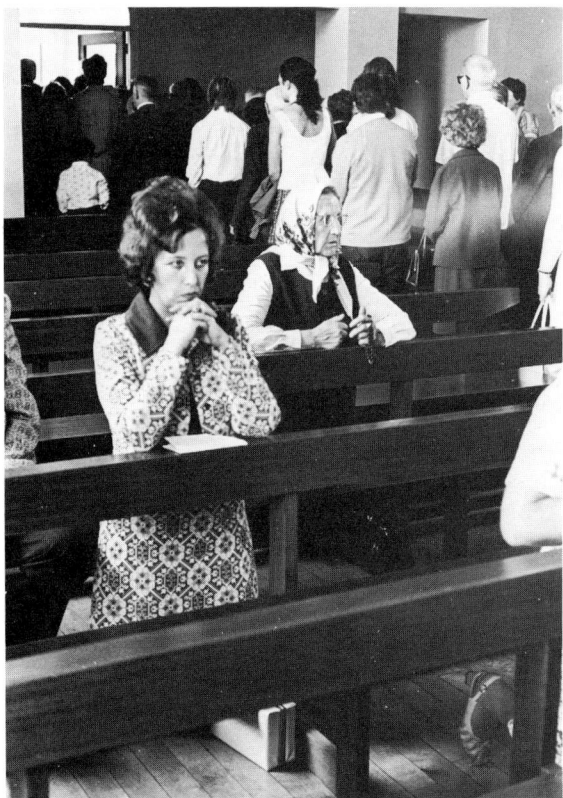

4

Muslim

The faith of Islam started in Arabia in the sixth century AD when a man called Muhammad brought the message to the people of the Arab tribes that there is only one God. Followers of this faith call Muhammad 'The Prophet' and worship this one God whom they call 'Allah'. These followers are called 'Muslims', a name which means 'those who submit to the will of Allah'.

Islam has spread since its beginnings in Arabia to many other countries and wherever there is a community of Muslims, you will almost certainly find a building set aside for worship. Such a building is known to Muslims as a Mosque. The word 'Mosque' means 'place of prostration'; prostration describes what the worshipper below is doing; it symbolises his wish, as a Muslim, to submit to the will of Allah.

In countries where Islam is the main religion, there are, of course, many Mosques. Muslims are expected to pray five times each day and they believe it is important to do this in company with other Muslims at a Mosque, whether it is in a Muslim country or a country like Britain.

In Britain, since there are not many Mosques it is not always possible for all Muslims to pray together. The Mosque has to serve all the Muslims who live in our community. We were told that some of those who worship regularly here have to travel four miles to join in the prayers.

If a Muslim finds he cannot attend the Mosque for prayers, he will say the prayers in his own home, or even at his place of work.

In the Mosque

Let us go inside the Mosque in our community and see how Muslims worship. We must first of all remove our shoes and leave them in the entrance hall. This is a mark of respect for the place of worship and is also because there are no seats in the room used for prayers but everyone sits on the floor.

A Room in Which to Wash

This room may seem strange for a place of worship, but the Muslim believes that he must go through a ceremony of washing before he prays, so a room is provided at the Mosque for this purpose. The **Qur'an**, the sacred book of the Muslims, says, 'Believers, when you rise to pray, wash your face and your hands as far as the elbows and wipe your hands and your feet to the ankle . . . Allah does not seek to burden you; he seeks only to purify you and to perfect his favour to you, so that you may give thanks.'

In this room for washing, the worshipper goes through a ritual of washing before prayers as follows:
(1) the hands are washed three times, including between the fingers;
(2) the mouth is washed out with water three times;
(3) the nose is washed with water and blown three times;
(4) the whole face is washed three times;
(5) both right and left hands are washed up to the elbow three times;
(6) the head is wiped with water;
(7) the ears are washed;
(8) both feet are washed up to the ankle.

The Place of Prayer

Come now from this room where the ritual washing takes place, into the main room at the Mosque, where the Imam, the leader of the Muslim community, leads the prayers.

Muslims all over the world, when they pray, always face towards Mecca, their holy city. Mecca is in Saudi Arabia and is a place where all Muslims hope to go on pilgrimage at least once in a lifetime. Every Mosque has a recess in the wall which marks the direction in which Mecca lies; this recess is called the **Mithrab**; in the Mosque in our

community, the Mithrab is in fact the bay window in this room, and it faces south-east.

The Imam told us that he, like many other Muslims, carries a special compass with him so that, wherever he is, he knows in which direction Mecca lies.

In the Mosque there are usually prayer mats on which the worshippers go through their prayer rite.

At the front of this room which is the place of prayer, you can see a series of steps. This is called the **Minbar** and is used like a pulpit from which the Imam, during Friday prayers, preaches a sermon. This idea of the Minbar is said to go back to the time of Prophet Muhammad himself, since he would choose a place with a few steps on which to speak, so that he could be seen and heard. Muslims say now that one step on the Minbar represents Muhammad's step and the others are for each of the Caliphs, i.e the early leaders of Islam, following the death of Muhammad.

When the Imam preaches the Friday sermon about midday, he stands on the Muhammad step. If he quotes from the Qur'an in his sermon, the quotation is in Arabic, the language of the sacred book, but otherwise the sermon is in the language of the people.

To one side of the Minbar there is a wooden stand on which the Qur'an is placed so that it may be recited to the worshippers.

Mosque Decoration
You will notice that there are no images, statues or even pictures of Muhammad or of anyone else in the Mosque. These are forbidden because the Muslim must worship Allah and only Allah; if there were representations of Muhammad or other human beings in the Mosque, he might be tempted to worship these.

Generally, a Mosque is specifically built as a place of worship and has a special design. Such Mosques are rectangular buildings with large open courtyards. In the centre of the courtyard there is often a fountain or tank for the worshipper to wash before prayers. The traditional Mosque has a domed roof and a minaret or tower from which the people are called to prayer five times each day. Often the walls of the Mosque are decorated with beautiful Arabic lettering and carefully designed patterns.

The Mithrab in the Mosque, pointing the direction of Mecca, has no decoration. This is so that there is nothing to distract the worshipper from his devotion to Allah.

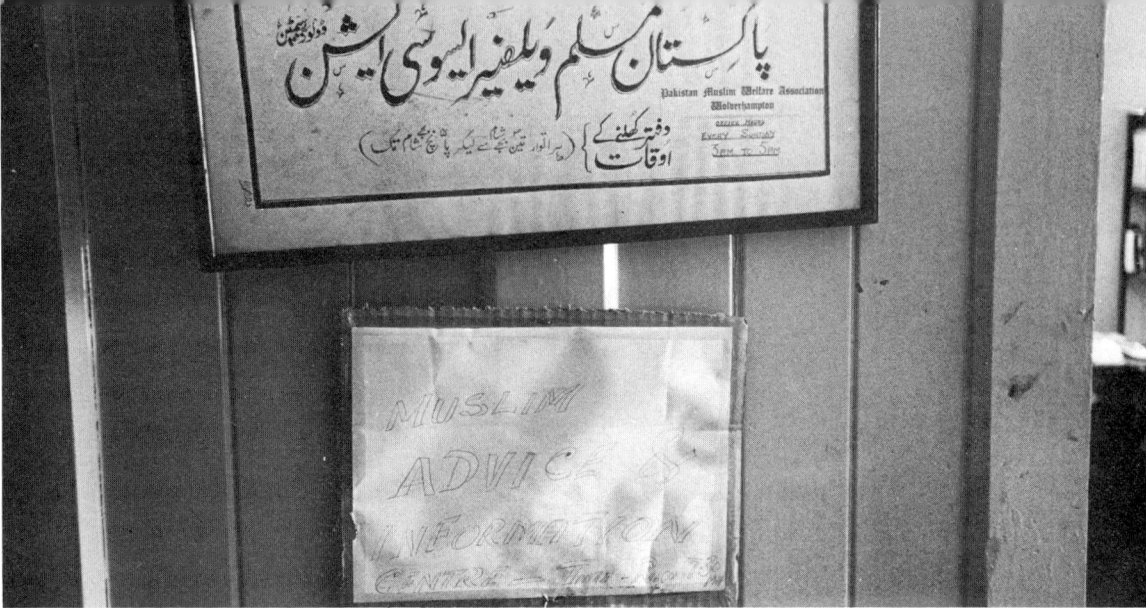

A Meeting Place for the Muslim Community

The Mosque in our town is very important to the Muslim community. They bought the building in 1969 and converted it into their Mosque. For them, it is not only a place of worship, but a meeting place for all members of the local Muslim community. There are rooms set aside for visitors, a kitchen so that food can be provided when necessary, and a room where Muslims may come for advice or information.

Children receive religious education at the Mosque. (You will discover more about this when you learn about sacred writings in worship.) The Imam teaches them Arabic so that they can read the Qur'an, their holy book; he also teaches them about the history of their religion.

Women normally say their prayers at home. However girls as well as boys do come to the Mosque to learn. Here one of them has been learning about the ninety-nine names which Muslims use to describe Allah. She is using these prayer beads to help her; there are thirty-three beads, so she works through the whole string three times, saying one of Allah's names, each time a bead passes through her fingers.

Here are the ninety-nine names for Allah:

the Merciful One	the Hearer	the Truth	the Governor
the Compassionate	He who sees	the Advocate	the Exalted
the King	the Judge	He who is strong	the Beneficient
the Holy One	the Just	He who is firm	the Forgiver
the Peace	the Kindly One	the Patron	the Avenger
the Faithful	the Well-informed	the Praiseworthy	He who pardons
the Overseer	the Forbearing	the Numberer	the Kindly One
the Mighty	the Great One	the Commencer	Ruler of the Kingdom
the Almighty	the Forgiving	the Restorer	Lord of Majesty and
the Justly Proud	the Grateful	the Life-giver	Generosity
the Creator	the High One	the Death-giver	the Equitable
the Maker	He who is great	the Living One	the Gatherer
the Fashioner	the Guardian	the Self-subsistent	the Rich One
the Pardoner	the Nourisher	the Discoverer	the Enricher
the Overcomer	the Reckoner	the Sublime	the Giver
the Bestower	the Majestic	the One	the Defender
the Provider	the Generous	the Eternal	the Distresser
the Opener	the Watcher	the Powerful	the Advantager
He who knows	He who answers	He who is able	the Light
the Restrainer	the Comprehensive	the Advancer	the Guide
the Extender	the Wise	the Retarder	the Incomparable
the Humbler	the Loving One	the First	He who abides
the Exalter	the Glorious	the Last	the Inheritor
the Empowerer	the Raiser (of the dead)	the Evident	the Director
the Baser	the Witness	the Hidden	the Long-suffering

Task 1
Imagine you are one of a group of
Muslims living in your town; you are
looking in the community for a suitable
building to use as a Mosque. Describe
what features it must have, if it is to
become a Mosque.

Task 2
Write a description of a traditional
Mosque; include the following words in
your account; Minbar, Mithrab, fountain,
domed roof, minaret, prayer mat.

Task 3
Write an imagined conversation between
a Muslim boy or girl and a Christian
friend, in which the Muslim explains
why it is important for the community to
have a Mosque.

Task 4
(a) Look at the photograph on page 30
of the prayer room in the Mosque.
Describe the objects you can see and their
use. Explain why the room is so bare.
(b) Look at the photographs on pages
29 and 30 of the room where the Muslim
washes before prayer; which of the eight
actions in the ritual washing described on
page 30 is the worshipper performing in
the photographs?

Task 5
If there is a Mosque near where you live,
ask your teacher to arrange a visit. Make
a list of questions to ask about the
planning and design of the Mosque and
its role in the life of the community.

5
Sikh

The Origin of the Sikh Faith

The Sikh faith began in the fifteenth
century as a result of the teachings of a
man called Nanak who lived in the
Punjab in North West India. Nanak grew
up as a Hindu but, since he lived in an
area where there were also many
Muslims, he had a knowledge of both
religions. When he was 30 years old
Nanak had a religious experience which
he later described as 'being taken to the
court of God'; in this, he felt he was
commanded to go and reveal God's
message to the world. He left his home
and with his friend Mardana he travelled
around India and neighbouring countries
telling people about God and how they
should live in order to please God. He
told men that it was not important
whether they were Hindu or Muslim
provided they believed in one God and
lived a good life.

He gained many followers who
gathered together to worship in what
came to be called a **Dharmsala**; this was
the earliest Sikh place of worship. In the
Dharmsala the early Sikhs, disciples of
Nanak, honoured God in prayer and
hymn singing. Towards the end of his life
Nanak settled down with his family and
some of his followers in a village called
Kartapur. He built a Dharmsala and
worshipped regularly. His followers
called him **Guru Nanak**; the word 'Guru'
means master or teacher. Sikhs look back
on a succession of ten Gurus starting

with Nanak whom you see at the centre of the picture. The others who succeeded him were:

Guru Angad, Guru Amar Das, Guru Ram Das, Guru Arjan Dev, Guru Hargobind, Guru Har Rai, Guru Har Krishan, Guru Teg Behadur, Guru Gobind Rai.

It was Guru Hargobind who renamed the Sikh place of worship and called it the **Gurdwara** which means 'the door of the Guru'.

Outside the Gurdwara

Wherever there is a Sikh community you will find a Gurdwara. The appearance of the Gurdwara varies; it may be a large, beautiful building or quite a small one; the form of the building itself is unimportant but what is important is that it contains a copy of the Sikh Holy Book, the *Guru Granth Sahib*.

Let us visit a local Gurdwara in our community. It is easily recognisable by its flagstaff flying the yellow flag which bears the emblem of the Sikh faith. Some Sikhs put their hands together and bow before it; perhaps they are remembering the ceremony in 1977 when this Gurdwara was first opened. An important Sikh leader came from India to perform the opening ceremony. It took place at 12 o'clock on a Sunday morning when the congregation gathered outside the Gurdwara. Some of them washed the flagstaff carefully because they believe that the flag of the Sikh faith must be respected. One of the ladies brought out the yellow flag with the Sikh symbol printed in black on it; the whole gathering chanted, 'Sat Sri Akal' three times: this is a traditional Sikh greeting which means 'God is truth' and reminds them of their loyalty to the one true God. The flagstaff was then placed in position and now the flag flies from it regularly, indicating that this is a Sikh Gurdwara.

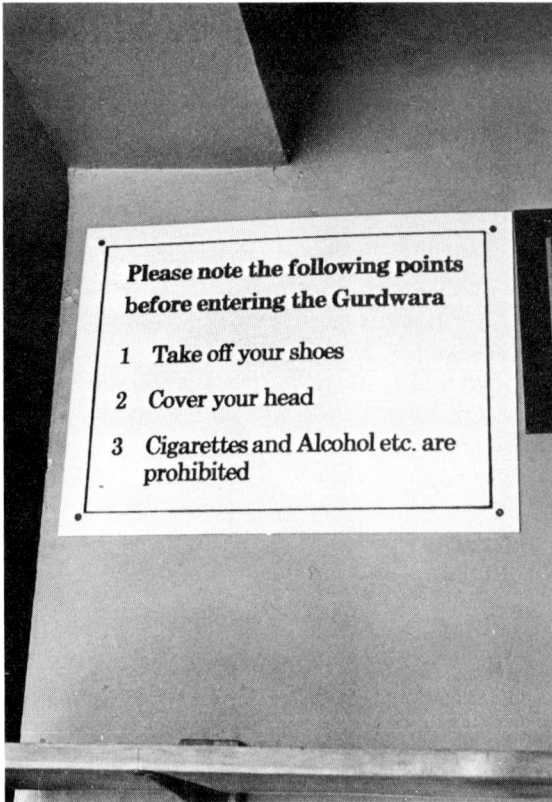

Please note the following points
before entering the Gurdwara

1 Take off your shoes

2 Cover your head

3 Cigarettes and Alcohol etc. are
   prohibited

right; this is not for any religious reason but simply that it is a traditional practice followed by the Sikhs. Taking care not to turn our backs on the Holy Book, we take our places on the floor. Immediately in front of us is an approach which leads to the Holy Book and there are vases of flowers arranged in front of where the book is kept. As we are settling down in our places on the floor, a Sikh lady enters and bows low before the Holy Book; we also notice that she places some money on the floor, near where the book is kept. After welcoming us to the Gurdwara we are given the opportunity to put questions to Mr Singh;

Inside the Gurdwara

Before entering the Gurdwara we see this notice. These are some of the rules observed by the Sikh community. As we enter we remove our shoes as a mark of respect, and place them either on the shelves in front of us or on the floor; we also cover our heads. We go straight to the most important room in the Gurdwara, the room which contains the Sikh Holy Book. Mr Singh is waiting to greet us and answer our questions.

Our attention is immediately drawn to a raised platform at the far end of which there are sliding glass doors and behind these doors is the Sikh Holy Book. Mr Singh asks us to sit down on the carpeted floor; there are no chairs and apart from pictures of some of the past teachers of the Sikh faith, the room is really quite bare. The boys and men must sit on the left and the girls and women on the

ਸਭ ਖੰਡਿ ਵਸੈ ਨਿਰੰਕਾਰੁ

Our question: Mr Singh, we notice that the lady who came in a few minutes ago placed some money on the floor: why did she do that?

Answer: People offer money or even food as a gift to God. The money is used to run the temple and we also try to send money to help other, poorer congregations.

If food is offered, it is used to make a sweet food called **Karah Parshad** which is given to everyone at the end of a service, or it may be used for a meal provided for worshippers at the Gurdwara in a room we call the **Langar**. I will show you this part of the Gurdwara later.

Our question: Why did the lady bow before making her offering?

Answer: She was bowing to our Holy Book, the Guru Granth Sahib. This is the most sacred article in the Gurdwara; it contains the words of the Gurus, the early teachers of the Sikh faith, and we regard it as our 'living Guru', to whom we can refer for guidance.

Our question: Can we look more closely at the Granth?

Answer: Yes indeed, but do not go inside the sliding doors; you see, anyone who approaches the Book must first have washed and put on clean clothing. The room you see to the left is a bathroom especially for this purpose.

Our question: Are there any other rules about the Holy Book?

Answer: You will notice that the people who worship here always sit lower than the Granth. The Book rests on cushions and is covered in embroidered covers which are called **Romallas**. Many Sikh ladies present the covers when there is a special occasion in their lives such as the birth of a child. Our Granth must be covered when it is not being read. Some Gurdwaras have a special room in which the Granth is placed every night; it is brought out to its place of honour each morning and when it is moved it is carried on the head.

Our question: Do all Gurdwaras keep the Granth behind sliding doors like these you have here?

Answer: No! That is simply a feature of this Gurdwara. Most keep the Holy Book under a canopy. This area behind the sliding doors is simply our form of a canopy and forms a special place for the sacred book.

Our question: Why is there a raised platform to one side of the Granth?

Answer: This part of the Gurdwara is used by the musicians. **Kirtan** is the word we use for hymn singing; the musicians sing hymns of the Gurus and such music is very important in our worship.

Our question: What else happens in a service of worship among the Sikhs?

Answer: We listen to readings from the Granth and someone may give a sermon. At the end of the service we all stand and join in a prayer called the **Ardas**. The **sangat**, that is the congregation, then receives a small portion of the sweet food which we call 'karah parshad': we eat it together to show that we are equal and united.

Our question: This building is quite large and there are many other rooms; what are these used for?

Answer: We have a library where people may study and there are rooms for visitors who may wish to stay the night. There is also a kitchen and an area for dining; this is the 'Langar' which I mentioned to you earlier.

Our question: When is the Gurdwara open for worship?

Answer: The Gurdwara is never closed and people are welcome to enter at any time. Services of worship take place from 6.30 pm onwards on most evenings. We also gather for worship on Sunday mornings and after our worship we share a meal in the Langar. Come with me now

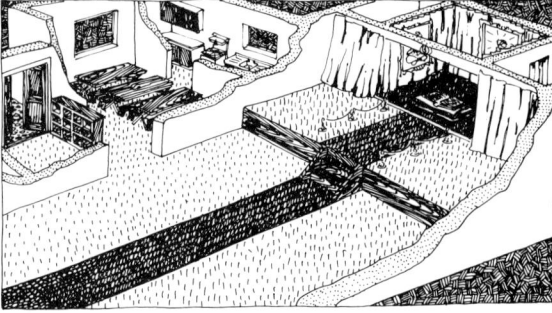
Plan of a Gurdwara

The Langar in the Gurdwara

An 'open-air' Langar

and I will show you the dining room. The word Langar really means 'communal kitchen'. The food which is brought to the Gurdwara by the congregation is prepared in the kitchen during worship and it is served in this area you see here.

Our question: Do other Gurdwaras have a Langar?

Answer: Yes indeed! As you know, Guru Nanak settled down to live in Kartapur and he started the tradition of Langar. He established one in Kartapur so that anyone who was hungry could come and eat. He also thought it important that all people, whatever their social position, should eat together. In some Gurdwaras, the Langar is in the open air, just outside the temple building.

Task 1
Draw the diagram of the Gurdwara and write a description of what happens in (a) the room used for worship and (b) the Langar. Use the photographs to help you with your descriptions.

Task 2
Imagine you are in charge of a party making a visit for the first time to a Gurdwara.

(a) Make a list of five instructions which you would give them before the visit.

(b) Make a list of three objects you would ask them to notice especially during the visit; give reasons for your choice.

Task 3
The following words have been used in this section:
Kirtan, Langar, Sangat, Gurdwara, Guru Granth Sahib, Romalla, Dharmsala.
Write the words and their meanings in your book.

The Golden Temple of Amritsar

When we were in the Langar we noticed hanging on the wall a photograph of a very beautiful building: we asked Mr Singh about it:

Our question: Is the building in that photograph a Sikh place of worship?

Answer: Yes! It is the Golden Temple of Amritsar. Amritsar is a special place for the Sikhs and it is regarded as the centre of our faith. Our fourth Guru, Guru Ram Das decided that the Sikhs needed a centre for worship and in 1577 he obtained some land and invited merchants and traders to come and live on it. Soon the population of the place grew and it was named the 'city of Amritsar' which means 'the pool of nectar'. The fifth Guru, Guru Arjan built this famous temple in the city.

Our question: Are all Gurdwaras in India like this one at Amritsar?

Answer: Oh no! It is more of a place of pilgrimage for Sikhs. The normal Sikh services of worship are not held in it and the Langar is completely separate from the temple itself. In the temple there is the Guru Granth Sahib and hymns are sung continuously. Visitors come from the early morning until late at night more or less every day. The temple is set in the centre of an artificial pool and has only one pathway leading to it so that everyone must use the same approach. The four doorways have steps leading down so that even the most important person must humble himself by stepping downwards before entering. The temple is covered with gold leaf so it is commonly called 'the Golden Temple'. The Sikhs call it the *Hari Mandir* which means 'the Lord's abode'. Pilgrims usually bathe in the water surrounding the temple before they enter.

Task 4

Write an imaginary interview between a boy who has just returned from a visit to Amritsar, and his school friend. Your interview should consist of at least five questions and answers about Amritsar.

The Golden Temple at Amritsar

Part II
Sacred Books in Worship

Introduction

Most religions have a book, or in some cases, books, which they regard as 'special' for their faith.

Such sacred books tell about God, and what he expects from people, how they should live and how they should worship. They usually also tell of the ideas of the founder of the particular faith, e.g. the Christian's New Testament includes information about the life and teaching of Jesus; the Sikh's *Guru Granth Sahib* contains the ideas of Guru Nanak and some of the other Gurus who succeeded him.

In most faiths there is some idea that their sacred book has been 'inspired' by God. This may mean that they believe God put the thoughts and ideas into the minds of those who wrote; for some followers of some of the faiths, it means that God 'dictated' the actual words and the writer simply wrote the words God put into his mind.

It is hardly surprising to find that in most faiths, when people meet for worship, at some point in the service, some part of the sacred book is read, and it may even be introduced in some of the faiths by words like, 'Hear the Word of God'. In this way, and sometimes by their own private reading of the sacred book, followers of the faith in question learn more about God and how they should live.

6

Hindu

Mr Bahri played a leading part in the worship at a Hindu temple. The occasion was the celebration of the birthday of Lord Rama, who is worshipped by many Hindus. As a part of their worship, a prayer of Lord Rama was being read.

Lord Rama

You have already learned about Vishnu, one of the greatest Gods of Hinduism. Krishna, you remember, is one of the ways in which Vishnu appeared among men.

Rama is believed to be another of the ways in which Vishnu appeared among men. Many Hindus hold nine days prayer, early in April, in memory of Lord Rama.

The most renowned story about Rama tells how he was the eldest son of his father, King Dasaratha. Rama had special powers and was given the task of destroying the evil demons troubling the world, especially the chief of the demons, Ravana.

Rama was married to a beautiful princess, Sita. King Dasaratha one day decided to give up his throne to one of his sons and go and live the life of a hermit. He chose Rama as his heir. Dasaratha had more than one wife, and the mother of one of his other sons, Bharata, was furious that her son had not been made heir. In the end, Dasaratha gave in to her; Bharata was made King and Rama

was banished. Sita insisted on sharing his troubles and they travelled together, dressed poorly, like hermits.

Rama did battle many times with demons. The demon king, Ravana, wanted to destroy Rama and win Sita for himself. One day he took the shape of a deer which Rama hunted. Ravana made him lose his way in the forest, then he

Ravana captures Sita

The story continues that Rama was suspicious and asked Sita if she had been faithful to him all this time. Sita was very upset and said that she would just as soon die if he did not still love and trust her. She asked Rama's brother, Lakshmana, to prepare a funeral pyre and she stepped on to it. Before the flames could harm·her, Agni, the fire God rescued her and told off Rama for mistrusting Sita.

All the evil forces had failed to destroy Rama and his loving wife, so this story is really saying that love is stronger than hate, good is stronger than evil.

The story of Rama and Sita comes from one of the Hindu Sacred Books. This story and other events in the life of the Lord Rama are remembered at the festival of Divali. This is the most popular of all festivals and it occurs once a year in October or November.

Hanuman

took the shape of a hermit and went to the house where Sita was living. Once inside he changed into his true shape with ten heads and twenty arms. He then carried Sita off to his palace in Sri Lanka.

Rama swore vengeance and set out to try and find Sita. He was helped by Hanuman, the monkey God of Hindu stories. Hanuman heard that Sita was in Sri Lanka. Since Sri Lanka is an island, and it was going to be difficult to get there from India, Hanuman leapt across the channel of water, found Sita and told her he would fetch Rama to rescue her. Ravana set Hanuman's tail on fire, but Hanuman used this to burn down Ravana's city. He and his monkeys formed a bridge over which Rama could cross to Sri Lanka and rescue Sita after killing Ravana.

43

The people celebrate by dancing at Divali. In the photographs Bijah is taking part in a dance to welcome back the Lord Rama. She is holding a Diva or light, for Divali is the festival of light, and hundreds of Divas can be seen at this time in Hindu homes.

Bijah's mother will have cleaned the house thoroughly and prepared special food for family and friends. New clothes will have been bought for the family and presents will be exchanged. Doorsteps will have been decorated with patterns in the hope that the family will have a prosperous New Year.

Hindu Sacred Books

Stories like the one which you have just read form a part of the contents of the Hindu Sacred Books. Stories about Rama are told in a very long Hindu book called Mahabharata and in another one called the Ramayana. One of the most important Hindu holy books is the Bhagavad-Gita, which is a part of the Mahabharata. The Bhagavad-Gita is about Lord Krishna who had long talks with Arjuna, showing him the path of duty and devotion.

The most ancient sacred books of the Hindus are the four Vedas which are mainly hymns in honour of the Gods. All these books are in Sanskrit, an ancient language no longer spoken except in acts of worship. An example of what it looks like appears on the next page.

Bijah

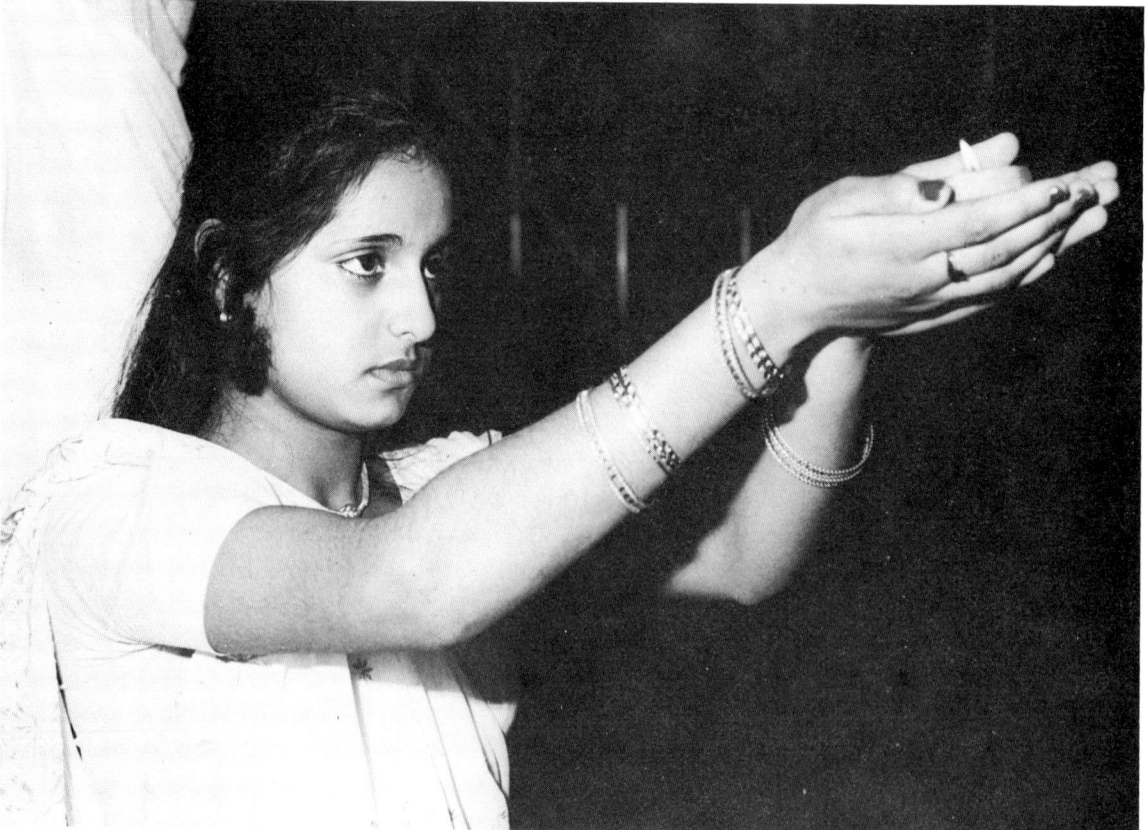

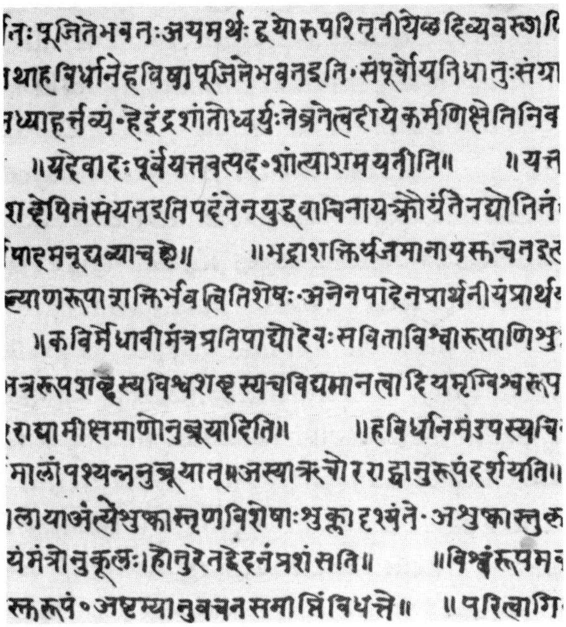

<!-- Sanskrit manuscript text (degraded, top-left) -->
निः पूजितेभवनः अयमर्थे द्र्या रूपरिततनीयश्चदिव्यव्रस्त्रानि
तथाहर्विधानेहविश्वापूजनेभवनइति संपूर्येयनिधानुःसंग्रा
ग्र्याहर्न्व्य-हइंद्रशांतीधर्व्युनेत्रनेल्दीयेकर्मणिसेनिनिव
।।यदेवदःपूर्वेयत्तत्रसद-शांत्याभमयत्नीनि।। ।।यन्त
शरृद्वितिसंयनरतितिपदेनेनयुद्वाबिनायक्र्यौर्येनेनघ्योनिनें
पारमनूव्याच्ह्ये॥ ॥भद्राशक्तिर्जमानाय्कन्चनरु
ह्यानरूपायशान्किर्भवलितिनिशेषः-अनेनपादेनप्रार्थनीयेप्रार्थे
॥कविर्मेधावीमंत्रप्रतिपादौरेःसविताविश्वरूपाणिष्
न्त्ररूपशब्द्स्यविश्वशब्दस्यचविद्यमानलादियमृग्भिश्वरूप
।राद्यामीस्माणोनुद्वयादिति।। ॥हविर्धनिमंउपस्थचि
मालांपश्यन्नुद्व्यात्॥अस्याक्रृरराद्वानुरूपदर्शयति।
।लायाअंतेषुक्राकृणणविशेषाःशुक्लदशंने-अश्वकान्लु
येमंत्रीनुकूलः।हानुरतेइदेरनंत्रशंसति॥ ॥विश्वंरूपमन
रूपं०अष्ठम्यानुव्रचनसमान्निविधत्ने॥ ॥परिलागि

Task 1

Study the photograph of Mr Bahri on page 42 carefully, and describe what you see.

Task 2

Make a list in your book of the different types of material to be found in the Hindu Sacred Books.

Task 3

Copy the following into your book, filling in the gaps:–

The Story of Rama

a Rama was given the task of ...
b Ravana, the Demon King, wanted ...
c He captured Sita by ...
d Ravana took Sita to ...
e Hanuman told Sita that ...
f When Ravana set Hanuman's tail on fire he ...
g Sita was upset after she had been rescued because ...
h Sita asked Lakshmana to ...
i She was saved by ...
j The story teaches that ...

Task 4

Draw a picture to illustrate a scene from the story.

Task 5

There are many similar interesting stories in the Hindu Sacred Books. Try to find one of these with the help of your teacher. You could write about it in your book or make up a play about it.

A chart of the main Hindu Sacred Books with a brief description

Book	Content	Date
The Vedas	Mainly hymns in honour of the Gods	1500–500 B.C.
The Upanishads	A collection of teachings of famous Hindus	1500–500 B.C.
Laws of Manu	Teaching on how men should behave	200–100 B.C.
Mahabharata	Stories of Gods and heroes of ancient times	400 B.C.–400 A.D.
Bhagavad-Gita (Part of Mahabharata)	Teachings of Lord Krishna	1–100 A.D.
Ramayana	Stories about the God, Rama	100–200 A.D.
Puranas	Descriptions of Gods and their activities	1–1000 A.D.

7
Jewish

Mr Alpren, at the time this photograph was taken, played a leading part in the local synagogue. He had been reading from the book which lies open before him. The book is not, in fact, a bible but a prayer book. A Jewish prayer book is full of passages from their scriptures.

The actual scriptures are usually read from scrolls similar to the one you see on page 18. The scrolls are kept behind a curtain which you see in the photograph on page 48. The place behind the curtain is called the **Ark**. The area in which Mr Alpren is sitting and from where the scroll is read is called the **Bimah**.

The Contents of the Scriptures

The scriptures play a very important part in Jewish worship in the synagogue and at home. The scripture of the Jews is basically the Old Testament, the first part of the Christian Bible. Jews divide their scriptures into three sections:

The Torah	The Prophets	The Writings
Genesis	Joshua	Psalms
Exodus	Judges	Proverbs
Leviticus	I Samuel	Job
Numbers	II Samuel	Song of Songs
Deuteronomy	I Kings	Ruth
	II Kings	Lamentations
	Isaiah	Ecclesiastes
	Jeremiah	Esther
	Ezekiel	Daniel
	and others,	Ezra
	known as	Nehemiah
	The Twelve	I Chronicles
	Prophets	II Chronicles

Task 1
With your teachers guidance, find out the main contents of the books of the Torah and write briefly about each one.

The language of the Jewish scriptures is Hebrew and Jews usually read in that language in their worship. Hebrew looks like this (it is read from right to left):

טַר־אַרְצְכֶם בְּעִתּוֹ יוֹרֶה וּמַלְקוֹשׁ וְאָסַפְתָּ דְגָנֶ

יִרֹשְׁךָ וְיִצְהָרֶךָ׃ וְנָתַתִּי עֵשֶׂב בְּשָׂדְךָ לִבְהֶמְתֶּ

וְכָלְתָ וְשָׂבָעְתָּ׃ הִשָּׁמְרוּ לָכֶם פֶּן־יִפְתֶּה לְבַבְכֶ

רְתֶּם וַעֲבַדְתֶּם אֱלֹהִים אֲחֵרִים וְהִשְׁתַּחֲוִיתֶם לָהֶם

זָרָה אַף־יְהֹוָה בָּכֶם וְעָצַר אֶת־הַשָּׁמַיִם וְלֹא

יֶה מָטָר וְהָאֲדָמָה לֹא תִתֵּן אֶת־יְבוּלָהּ וַאֲבַדְתֶּ

47

The Ark (closed)

The Ark (open)

Taking The Scroll From The Ark

It is an honour to remove the scroll from the Ark. The curtain is gently pulled back to reveal the scrolls. The congregation is standing and as the Ark is opened, repeats words which end

'Blessed be he who in his holiness gave the Law to his people Israel'.

The scroll is carefully lifted out from the Ark and given to the Reader. As he takes it, he and the congregation say,

'Hear, O Israel; the Lord our God, the Lord is One. One is our God: Great is our Lord: Holy is his name.'

The scroll is dressed with bells and a breastplate and a pointer. The bells and breastplate are reminders of the High Priest of ancient Judaism who had these as part of his dress. The pointer is used by the Reader to follow the lines as he reads.

The scroll is carried reverently to the Bimah and laid on the desk. As it is placed on the desk, the Reader says 'and may he help, shield and save all who trust in him, and let us say "Amen". Ascribe all of you greatness unto your God and render honour to the Law.'

Before the reading begins, the Reader says, 'Bless ye the Lord who is to be blessed'. The congregation responds, 'Blessed be the Lord who is to be blessed for ever and ever. Blessed art thou, O Lord, our God, King of the Universe, who hast chosen us from all peoples and hast given us thy Law. Blessed art thou, O Lord, who givest the Law'.

48

Task 2

Copy the plan of the synagogue into your book using a full page. At the Ark, Bimah and seats for the congregation, write in the words spoken at that point in the procession.

Task 3

Using what you can see in the photographs in this section and what you have read, write a paragraph about how important the scriptures are to Jews and how they treat them with the greatest respect.

A Festival – Simcha Torah

The Torah is so divided that during the course of a year the whole of it will be read in the synagogue services. There are also set passages from the Prophets which relate to each passage from the Torah and these usually follow the reading from the Torah in worship.

The Jewish festival, **Simcha Torah** i.e. Rejoicing of the Law, is concerned with the scriptures. On the evening before the festival, the passage which completes the reading of the Torah for the year is read in the synagogue – i.e. a section from the closing chapters of Deuteronomy. This special occasion is usually preceded by a procession in which the sacred scrolls are carried round the synagogue with children following and singing happy songs.

The next morning, there is another similar procession in the synagogue and the scripture reading begins with the same passage as on the previous evening, followed by the first reading for the new year of readings, i.e. the first chapter of the book of Genesis.

Task 4

You are asked by a friend about what happens at Simcha Torah; describe what it is all about and what takes place. Tell him also what the two readings are about – the last chapter of Deuteronomy and the first chapter of Genesis.

Plan of a synagogue

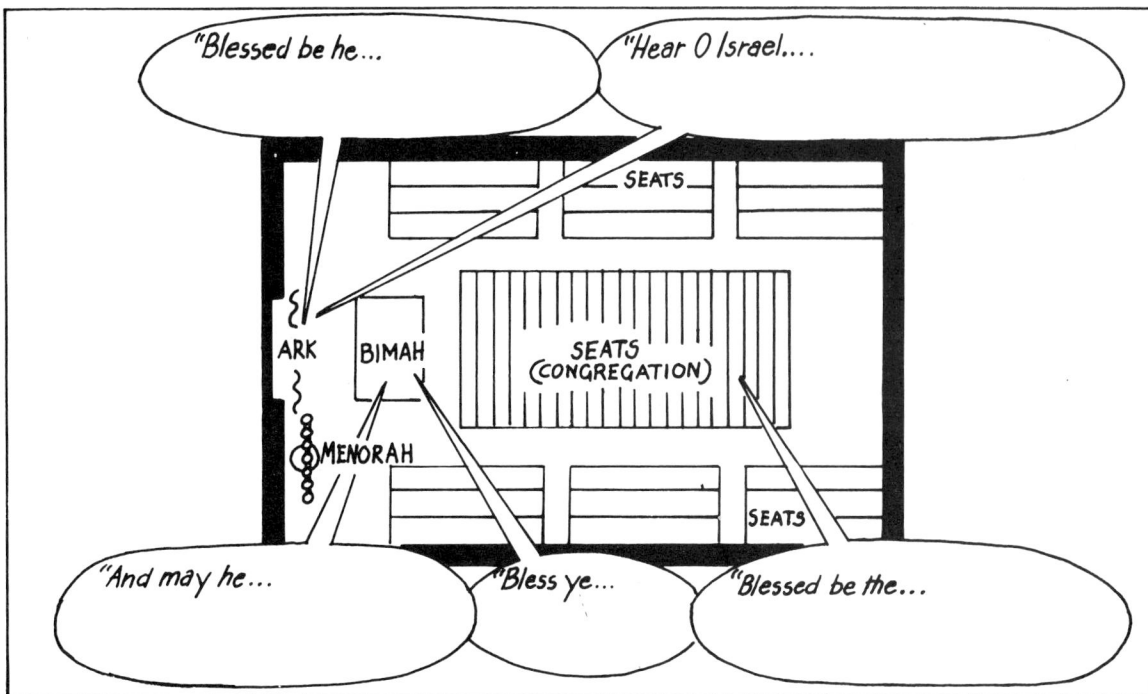

8

Christian

Mr Hyman Harris, is a Deacon in the Baptist Church to which he belongs. (A Deacon is one of several people appointed to help the Minister of the church.) He is here reading the scriptures to the congregation in a service of worship.

We spoke to Mr Harris about the Bible:

Our question: Mr Harris, how important has the Bible been in your life?

Answer: When I was a child, back in Kingston, Jamaica, I spent a lot of time with my grandfather, who was blinded in an accident. The Bible was very important to him, and since he could not read it for himself, I used to read it to him when I had learned to read. As I grew up, its message about Jesus Christ became very important to me and has provided me with the guidance I need to live a satisfying life.

Our question: Why are you reading the Bible in the service of worship?

Answer: It is the custom of my church, and most other Christian churches, for someone like myself and not just the Minister to read the scriptures in the service. This is an important part of our worship because it reminds us of our faith and the teaching of Jesus which we try to follow.

Our question: What part of the Bible were you reading when the photograph was taken?

Answer: I was reading from the first letter to the Corinthians, chapter 13, a very well known chapter to Christians, because it speaks about love.

Our question: Is that important to you?

Answer: It certainly is! I believe that the most important thing we learn from the Bible is that God loves, and Jesus said we ought also to love one another.

Our question: How do you feel when you read the Bible in a service of worship?

Answer: I feel that it is a great honour and privilege to be able to share in worship in this way: indeed, I always feel it is a privilege to read the Bible whether I am reading to the congregation in worship or whether I am reading it quietly by myself at home.

The Bible

The scriptures of Christians are to be found in the Bible. This contains two main sections: (a) the Old Testament which is also the scripture of the Jews. Jesus, the founder of Christianity, was, of course, a Jew and the Christian church grew out of a background of Judaism. (b) The New Testament.

The New Testament

The New Testament is especially important to Christians. It is made up of a collection of writings of various kinds:
Gospels – an account of the life and teaching of Jesus.
The Acts of the Apostles – an account of the growth of the early church.
Letters – sent to various churches and individual people in the first century AD.
Revelation – a rather strange book of visions.

The original language of the New Testament is Greek, because when it was first written, Greek was the language which would be understood by people who could read in most parts of the Roman Empire. Below is part of the New Testament in Greek.

Translations have been made, using the oldest Greek manuscripts available. Here is a page from a manuscript which dates to the fourth century; it is called the **Codex Sinaiticus**. You can see this in the British Museum in London.

Codex Sinaiticus

Ὁ θεὸς ἀγάπη ἐστίν, καὶ ὁ μένων ἐν τῇ ἀγάπῃ ἐν τῷ θεῷ μένει καὶ ὁ θεὸς ἐν αὐτῷ μένει. **17** ἐν τούτῳ τετελείωται ἡ ἀγάπη μεθ' ἡμῶν, ἵνα παρρησίαν ἔχωμεν ἐν τῇ ἡμέρᾳ τῆς κρίσεως, ὅτι καθὼς ἐκεῖνός ἐστιν καὶ ἡμεῖς ἐσμεν ἐν τῷ κόσμῳ τούτῳ. **18** Φόβος οὐκ ἔστιν ἐν τῇ ἀγάπῃ, ἀλλ' ἡ τελεία ἀγάπη ἔξω βάλλει τὸν φόβον, ὅτι ὁ φόβος κόλασιν ἔχει, ὁ δὲ φοβούμενος οὐ τετελείωται ἐν τῇ ἀγάπῃ. **19** ἡμεῖς ἀγαπῶμεν, ὅτι αὐτὸς πρῶτος ἠγάπησεν ἡμᾶς. **20** ἐάν τις εἴπῃ ὅτι Ἀγαπῶ τὸν θεόν, καὶ τὸν ἀδελφὸν αὐτοῦ μισῇ, ψεύστης ἐστίν· ὁ γὰρ μὴ ἀγαπῶν τὸν ἀδελφὸν αὐτοῦ ὃν ἑώρακεν, τὸν θεὸν ὃν οὐχ ἑώρακεν οὐ δύναται ἀγαπᾶν. **21** καὶ ταύτην τὴν ἐντολὴν ἔχομεν ἀπ' αὐτοῦ, ἵνα ὁ ἀγαπῶν τὸν θεὸν ἀγαπᾷ καὶ τὸν ἀδελφὸν αὐτοῦ.

Task 1

Find in your Bible, the passage that Mr Harris was reading – 1 Corinthians: chapter, 13 verses 1–7. Read it carefully and you will see that the theme of the passage is love.

Write a few sentences saying what qualities you would expect to find in Mr Harris if he tries to put the teaching of this chapter about love into practice in his life. (It may help you to know that he worked for many years in a factory, but he is now retired.)

Task 2

Write in your book, the heading 'The New Testament'. Using the list of contents at the beginning of your Bible, list the books of the New Testament in three columns as below:

Gospels   Letters   Others

The Bible in Church

It would be very unusual indeed if you attended a service of worship in a Christian church and did not hear the Bible being read at some point in the service. The Gospels, especially, are important since they give accounts of the life and teaching of Jesus and Christians believe that here they will find guidance about how to live life.

You might, however, go into two different Christian churches and hear the same passage from the Bible being read and not at once recognise it as the same passage. This is because there are many translations of the Bible in English. Here are some of the versions in common use today:

The Authorised Version – 1611
The Revised Standard Version – 1946
The New English Bible – 1961
The Good News Bible – 1976.

Pastor Joseph is a Minister of a Christian group called 'The New

Testament Church of God'. In the photograph he is emphasising what he is reading from the New Testament by raising his arms. The worshippers are following the reading in their copy of the Bible. The version he is using is the Authorised Version which was published in the year 1611; this is still a very popular edition of the Bible with many Christians.

The Reverend John Fielding is a Minister of a Methodist church. He is also reading from the Bible in a service of worship, but he is using the more recently published version – the New English Bible.

Both these men are reading the same passage from the New Testament – the Parable of the Good Samaritan from Luke: Chapter 10, verses 25–37.

In the Authorised Version, which Pastor Joseph is using, it reads as follows:

25 And, behold, a certain lawyer stood up, and tempted him, saying, Master, what shall I do to inherit eternal life?

26 He said unto him, What is written in the law? how readest thou?

27 And he answering said, Thou shalt love the Lord thy God with all thy heart, and with all thy soul, and with all thy strength, and with all thy mind; and thy neighbour as thyself.

28 And he said unto him, Thou hast answered right: this do, and thou shalt live.

29 But he, willing to justify himself, said unto Jesus, And who is my neighbour?

30 And Jesus answering said, A certain *man* went down from Jerusalem to Jericho, and fell among thieves, which stripped him of his raiment, and wounded *him*, and departed, leaving *him* half dead.

31 And by chance there came down a certain priest that way: and when he saw him, he passed by on the other side.

32 And likewise a Levite, when he was at the place, came and looked *on him*, and passed by on the other side.

33 But a certain Samaritan, as he journeyed, came where he was: and when he saw him, he had compassion *on him*.

34 And went to *him*, and bound up his wounds, pouring in oil and wine, and set him on his own beast, and brought him to an inn, and took care of him.

35 And on the morrow when he departed, he took out two pence, and gave *them* to the host, and said unto him, Take care of him; and whatsoever thou spendest more, when I come again, I will repay thee.

36 Which now of these three, thinkest thou, was neighbour unto him that fell among the thieves?

37 And he said, He that shewed mercy on him. Then said Jesus unto him, Go and do thou likewise.

In the New English Bible, which the Reverend John Fielding is using, it reads as follows:

ON ONE OCCASION a lawyer came forward to put this test question to him: 'Master, what must I do to inherit eternal life?' Jesus said, 'What is written in the Law? What is your reading of it?' He replied, 'Love the Lord your God with all your heart, with all your soul, with all your strength, and with all your mind; and your neighbour as yourself.' 'That is the right answer,' said Jesus; 'do that and you will live.'

But he wanted to vindicate himself, so he said to Jesus, 'And who is my neighbour?' Jesus replied, 'A man was on his way from Jerusalem down to Jericho when he fell in with robbers, who stripped him, beat him, and went off leaving him half dead. It so happened that a priest was going down by the same road; but when he saw him, he went past on the other side. So too a Levite came to the place, and when he saw him, he went past on the other side. But a Samaritan who was making the journey came upon him, and when he saw him was moved to pity. He went up and bandaged his wounds, bathing them with oil and wine. Then he lifted him on to his own beast, brought him to an inn, and looked after him there. Next day he produced two silver pieces and gave them to the innkeeper, and said, "Look after him; and if you spend any more, I will repay you on my way back." Which of these three do you think was neighbour to the man who fell into the hands of the robbers?' He answered, 'The one who showed him kindness.' Jesus said, 'Go and do as he did.'

Task 3
Read both versions of the parable of the Good Samaritan carefully. Write a few sentences saying, with reasons, which version you prefer.

Task 4
Pastor Joseph is obviously emphasising what he is reading. Which part of the parable do you think he is reading in the photograph, which makes him feel he must emphasise its importance to the congregation? Give reasons for your answer and write out the part of the parable you have chosen.

Task 5
Today translations are available in hundreds of languages so that people of many lands can read and understand the Bible for themselves. There was, however, a time when few people, even in this country, were educated. An early attempt to give the Bible to such people who could not read very well was known as the **Hieroglyph Bible**. It consisted of small pictures with a few words of the text printed round them. Here is an example of how it looked:

Using this example to guide you, design a page for such a Bible, telling the story of the Good Samaritan.

Another of the ways in which the Christian scriptures appear in some churches is that quite often a story or incident from the Bible is the theme of a stained glass window. Such windows add considerable beauty and colour to many churches, but, many years ago they also served another useful purpose; they helped to teach people about the Christian faith at a time when many of them could not read.

The window you see here tells about the story of Jesus and the Samaritan Woman. You can read this in John: chapter 4, verses 1 to 42.

Task 6
Use tracing paper to copy the window; you can then colour in your copy and if you place it on the classroom window you will see it as it appears in Church.

9

Muslim

Mr Shah is the Imam for the local Muslim community. Part of his responsibility is to teach at the Mosque and he has been appointed by the Mosque Committee. In order to take the position of Imam he has to know a great deal about the **Qur'an**, the holy book of the Muslims. Part of his task is to teach Arabic, since the Qur'an is written in this language. He has to be able to express himself and show his knowledge of Islam, because on Sundays and Fridays he conducts prayer and preaches. In his sermon, he may use the Holy Qur'an or the **Hadith**, which is a book which contains collections of the sayings and doings of Muhammad, the prophet who is the Messenger of God to the Muslims.

The Imam

The Qur'an

The word Qur'an means 'recitation'. It is believed that God sent the messages contained in the Qur'an to Muhammad through the Angel Gabriel over a period of twenty years. This began while Muhammad was meditating in the Cave of Hira near Mecca in AD 610 when according to Muslim tradition, the Angel Gabriel appeared to him for the first time.

The Angel handed Muhammad the scroll and told him to read the words on it. Muhammad replied that he could not read but the Angel insisted and finally Muhammad was able to read aloud the words on the scroll: 'In the Name of Allah, the Beneficient, the Merciful, read! In the Name of Allah who creates man from a clot of blood, read! And your Lord is the most Bountiful, who teaches by the pen, teaches man what he did not know before.' These words are in the first **sura**, or chapter of the Qur'an. Afterwards Muhammad had many other visions. He recited the information given to him by Allah to his followers. After his death, all of his recitations were collected together and so the Qur'an was produced.

Muslims believe that the Qur'an is the word of Allah and since Muhammad lived in Arabia it was given to him in the Arabic language, an example of which you can see below.

Children learning Arabic

Studying the Qur'an

Muslims learn the prayers and some short chapters by heart. Translations of the Holy Book are not usually allowed in the Mosque, so it is important for Muslim children to learn Arabic. The Qur'an has one hundred and fourteen chapters. They tell men that there is only one God, whom they call Allah, and all men are to serve him. The Qur'an also tells people how to behave and deals with questions of marriage, war, work and property. In fact, it deals with every aspect of life and is a guide to how a true Muslim must live.

Task 1
As a parent of one of the boys in the picture, tell why you have sent your child to the Mosque and say what you think he will learn. Use the heading, 'the religious education of a Muslim'.

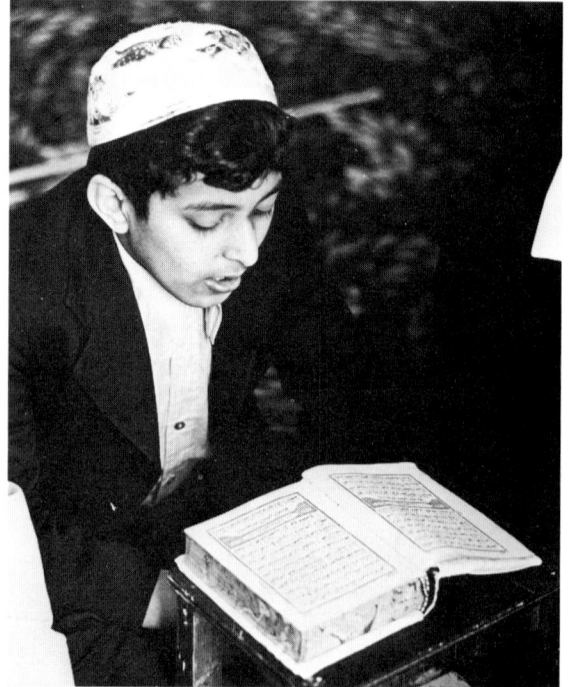

58

Task 2
Study the photographs on pages 56 and 58 and answer the questions:

(a) What language is written on the blackboard?

(b) Why is this language used?

(c) What do you think the boys in the photographs are doing.

(d) What do you notice about the dress of the boys and the Imam?

(e) What is missing which you would find in your classroom?

Task 3
Tell how Muhammad received the Qur'an.

Studying the Qur'an
The children are studying the Qur'an. They believe that every word of the Qur'an is the word of Allah and that it has been preserved, word for word, as it was revealed to Muhammad. They are taught that it is the last and final book sent by Allah and that it will always be preserved. They will grow up to read the Qur'an every day and will try to follow its teaching in their lives.

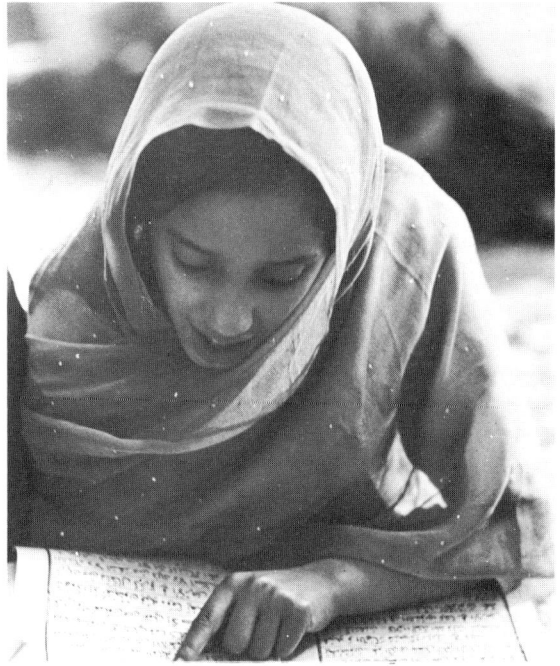

Studying the Qur'an

Every chapter in the Qur'an except one, begins with the words 'in the Name of Allah, the Compassionate, the Merciful.' You will see these words in Arabic on page 57 (bottom line, right hand page).

ALLAH

بِاللَّهِ

Each chapter, which is called a sura, has a name according to some person or topic mentioned in it: e.g. Man, Daybreak, Comfort, the Sun, the Pen, Muhammad, Women, the Unbelievers. The Qur'an is approximately the same length as the Christian's New Testament. It is said to be easy to learn in Arabic and some Muslims can recite all of it by heart. No one must read it or touch it without first washing. When it is being read it is often kept on a stand. As a mark of respect for the sacred book it may be kept in a special embroidered cover. Before he reads, the reader touches his head with the book and kisses the cover.

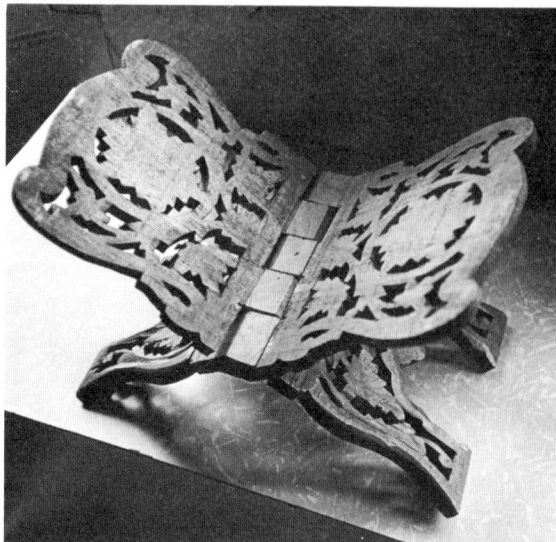

Passages from the Qur'an about the Qur'an

The Qur'an has been composed by none other than Allah, it is undoubtedly from the Lord of the Creation.

These are the revelations of the Qur'an, the Glorious Book, a guide and joyous news to true believers who pray regularly.

The Qur'an has come from the One who is wise and all knowing.

This Qur'an is a guide and blessing to true believers.

We have made the Qur'an easy to remember.

We have revealed the Qur'an in the Arabic language that you may be able to grasp its meaning. It is a copy of our eternal book, which is full of wisdom.

This is revealed by the Compassionate, the Merciful – it brings good news and warnings.

To those who truly believe, it guides and heals.

This book is revealed by Allah, the Mighty One, the One who knows everything, who forgives sin and accepts repentance.

If all the trees in the earth were pens, and the sea, with seven more seas to replenish it, were ink, the writing of Allah's words could never be finished. Mighty is Allah and wise.

Whenever the Qur'an is being recited listen to it quietly so that you may receive mercy.

Passages from the Qur'an About How To Live

Be patient, just as those messengers who were steadfast were patient.

Do not treat men with scorn, nor walk proudly on earth: Allah does not love the arrogant. Be modest in the way you walk and lower your voice: the ugliest sound is a donkey's braying.

Re-pay evil with something that is finer.

If an evil-doer brings you a piece of news enquire first into its truth, lest you should wrong others unwittingly.

Believers, let no man make fun of another man, who may perhaps be better than himself.

Show kindness to your parents and to your kindred, to the orphans and to the needy, to your near and distant neighbours. Allah does not love conceited and boastful men, nor those who are tight-fisted and encourage others to be stingy also.

Do not allow your hatred for other men to turn you away from justice.

Believers, liquor and gambling, are only a filthy work of Satan; avoid them so that you may prosper.

Task 4

Imagine you are either the boy or the girl in the photographs on pages 58 and 59 and you are being interviewed about the Qur'an; write down the following questions and provide your answers to them. The information on pages 59 to 61 will help you. Use the heading 'an interview with a Muslim'.

(a) How does each chapter of the Qur'an begin?

(b) I know you call Allah 'Lord of the Creation'; tell me five other qualities you believe he has.

(c) From whom did the Muslims receive the Qur'an?

(d) What does the Qur'an give to true believers?

(e) Why is it written in Arabic?

(f) In what way does a study of the Qur'an help you in life?

Task 5

From what you have learned about the Qur'an, write a brief description of the character of a Muslim who closely follows its teaching in his life.

10
Sikh

Mr Ayaib Singh is sitting cross-legged behind a large book which is lying on a decorated cushion. You can find this in any Sikh temple (Gurdwara), whether it is in Britain or in India, where the Sikh religion began. The place of honour is given to this book and the worshippers treat it with the greatest respect.

Everyone stands and bows before it, if it is moved from its position. You remember when we were looking at places of worship, the Gurdwara we visited had the Holy Book behind sliding doors; in this Gurdwara, Mr Singh sits with the book under a decorated canopy so that this becomes the most important feature in the Gurdwara.

Beside Mr Ayaib Singh stands Mr Jurchann Singh, waving a **chauri**, which consists of animal hair bound to a wooden or metal handle. This custom has become another mark of respect for the Holy Book. Notice that Mr Ayaib Singh, who reads the book, is on a level with it, not standing over it – because the book is more important in worship than he is. The book is called the **Adi Granth** i.e. 'original book'; it is also known as the **Guru Granth Sahib** i.e. 'Lord teacher book'. Whenever a Sikh worshipper enters the Gurdwara he kneels, and bows low with his forehead on the ground, before the Guru Granth Sahib. He then stands with folded hands, his head bowed and he murmers **waheguru** i.e. 'Wonderful Lord'. Before entering the Gurdwara, as a further mark of respect for the book, he has removed his shoes.

The book must be kept open when a congregation is assembled and someone, like Mr Ayaib Singh, known as the **Granthi** must sit behind it; when it is not being read, however, it is covered with a sheet and after worship it is wrapped in several covers.

The importance of the Guru Granth Sahib is emphasised by the fact that when a new Gurdwara is opened there is a special ceremony at which the book is placed in position. On some special occasions, such as the birthday of a Guru, or the anniversary of the death of a Guru, the whole of the Granth may be read continuously by a team of readers. This takes about forty-eight hours. At a Sikh wedding the sacred book is particularly important, since it is thought to be the only necessary witness to the marriage. If the book is not present then the religious ceremony cannot take place. In one of the Gurdwaras in our community the special canopy which we see below is set aside for marriage ceremonies.

Task 1

The picture below shows Guru Nanak, the founder of the Sikh faith, with his friend, Bala, at his side, waving a chauri of palm leaves and feathers. This would keep the Guru cool and keep flies away from him; it also signifies respect for the Guru as a man of authority. The branches of the tree act as a canopy over their heads.

(a) Compare this with the treatment given to the Guru Granth Sahib in a Sikh temple today.

(b) Draw a picture of the canopy under which the Guru Granth Sahib is kept in the Gurdwara.

The Origin of the Granth

The book is a collection of writings by a number of people, including Guru Nanak, some Hindu and Muslim teachers and Guru Arjan who put most of it together. Guru Gobind Singh stated that other writings were to be included in the book and declared that there was to be no living Guru to succeed him; from the time of his death, the Guru Granth Sahib would be the leader and guide of the Sikhs.

The book is made up of 5894 hymns or poems all of which can be chanted to music. The Guru Granth Sahib is written in the Punjabi language which looks like this:

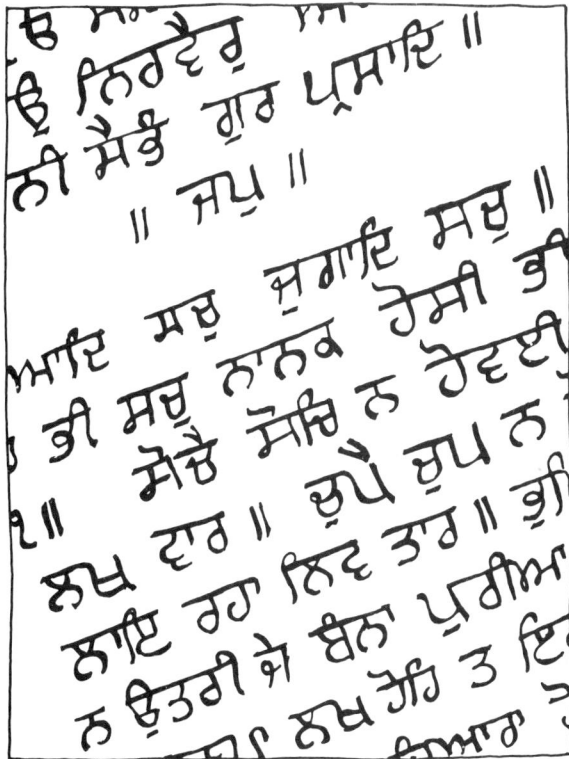

These are in fact the opening words of the Guru Granth Sahib and are referred to as the **Mool Mantra** i.e. the basic or perfect sacred chant. In translation it means:

'There is one God,
Eternal Truth is His Name,
Maker of all things,
Fearing nothing and at enmity with nothing,
Timeless is His Image,
Not begotten, being of His own Being,
By the grace of the Guru, made known to men.'

These opening words are followed by what is usually regarded as the most important part of the book, the **Japji** which means 'remembrance'. The Japji is used every day by the Sikh worshipper in his morning prayers.

Task 2
Using the pictures as a guide, draw a diagram showing the Guru Granth Sahib under its canopy and the Granthi behind it; show also the position of the worshippers in relation to the book.

Task 3
What can you learn from the photographs in this section which suggests that the Guru Granth Sahib is treated with the greatest respect?

Task 4
Write a sentence or two about each of the following:
   (a) Guru Granth Sahib
   (b) The Granthi
   (c) The Chauri
   (d) Gurdwara
   (e) The Mool Mantra
   (f) The Japji

Task 5
Describe any similarities you see between the two men in the photographs on pages 62 and 63.
Do you think they are proud of their jobs in worship?
Why do you think it is an honour to carry out such duties?

Part III
Prayer in Worship

Introduction

A place of worship is sometimes described as a 'Place of Prayer'; this would not be a complete description but it would, nevertheless, say something important about what goes on in such a place. Worship in all the world's major faiths involves prayer in some form or another.

What image came into your mind as you read that word, 'prayer'? Someone kneeling with hands together? Someone standing with hands raised towards the sky? You may also have various ideas in your mind about what makes up a prayer; making a request to God? Confessing that you have done something wrong? Offering thanks to God? We will discover that all these images and ideas which come to mind may be right since prayer, in whatever faith we are considering, has many forms and many ways of being expressed. It may be telling God you want to follow his teaching; it may be telling him you are sorry for something wrong; it may be asking him for something you feel is important to you; it may simply be telling him how wonderful you believe him to be.

The words may be spoken aloud, or they may simply be thoughts in the mind, or they may be sung or chanted as a hymn; the prayer may be offered in a place of worship, or anywhere else on earth; it may be thought out carefully and quietly, or it may be someone else's words you are reading or reciting; it may be an urgent cry from the heart. However it is phrased and wherever it is offered, it is an important part of man's approach to the God in whom he believes and whom he wishes to serve.

11
Hindu

You have already learned something about Hindu worship and know that prayer is a regular part of it. Such prayer will take place either in a temple or at home but in both cases, it will usually be offered before a shrine which consists of statues and pictures of some of the Hindu gods, for example, Rama and Krishna, who are represented in the forms you see here.

Rama

Krishna

We have already noted that sometimes in a Hindu home a complete room may be used as a temple and here the family and probably their friends meet for worship. Even although it is a room in a house, it is treated as a holy place and anyone entering removes his shoes before doing so.

You remember that there is such a temple in the home of the Patel family where Mr and Mrs Patel and their children regularly worship every day, but on some occasions each week are joined by many Hindu friends who worship with them.

Chanting Prayers

Much of their worship consists of prayers which are chanted to Indian music which is often played on a harmonium. These chanted prayers are called **Bhajans**. Here are two examples of these; they are of course chanted in one of the Indian languages and if you read the left hand column you will get some idea of how it sounds.

Here is such an occasion when the family is joined by many of the friends who regularly use this temple as their place of worship.

Vahe Guru Vahe Guru Vahe Guru Ji Bolo	Hail and chant the Guru's name
Sathya Nam Sathya Nam Sathya Nam Ji Bolo	Chant the name of Sathya
Nithya Nithya Japiye There Nam Ji Bolo	Always recite his name
Sathya Nam Sathya Nam Sathya Nam Ji Bolo	Chant the name of Sathya
Ram Ram Ram Ram Ram Ram Ji Bolo	Hail and chant Rama's name
Nithya Nithya Japiye Ram Nam Ji Bolo	Always recite the name of Rama
Krishna Krishna Krishna Krishna Krishna Ji Bolo	Hail and chant Krishna's name
Nithya Nithya Hapiye Krishna Nam Ji Bolo	Always recite the name of Krishna
Siva Siva Siva Siva Siva Nam Ji Bolo	Hail and chant Siva's name. (Sathya is a name used of various Hindu gods and means 'true', 'real')
Antarjyoti Namo	I bow to the Inner Light
Paramatma Jyoti Namo	I bow to the Light of the Supreme Spirit
Akhanda Jyoti Namo	I bow to the One Unbroken Light
Mama Jeevana Jyoti Namo	I bow to the Light of my Life
Antaryami Namo Jai	I bow to the Inner Self (residing in the heart)

69

Task 1

(a) Imagine you are the worshipper shown here: you are being asked the following questions; write out the questions and follow each one with your answer.

1 Before you stepped into the room which is the temple did you prepare in any way for worship?

2 You appear to be looking at the shrine as you worship; in what way does this help you in your prayers?

3 Can you tell me a little about one of the gods you are looking at in the shrine?

4 Describe what you and your fellow worshippers are doing when you are chanting the Bhajans.

5 Describe the instrument which provides the music in your worship. In what way does this help your prayers?

(b) Copy out the first Bhajan into your book. You may think that the last line is missing; write in what you think it would be both in the Indian version and in the English.

70

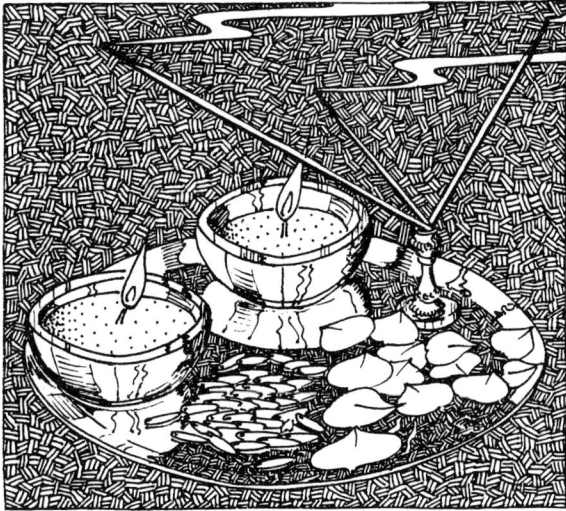
Arti tray

Puja

Puja is the Hindu name for an act of worship. It is a Sanskrit word, and it means honour or reverence given to the gods.

This act of worship is often offered at the beginning of the day but whenever it takes place the worshipper will have taken a bath and put on clean clothes as a mark of respect for the god. In this worship an **arti** tray or prayer plate is important.

Perhaps the most important items on such a tray are the lamps which symbolise the presence of God. These are called **divas**. They are usually made from flour and water mixed together to form a dough; a hole is made in the centre and cotton wool is placed inside to act as a wick, oil is poured on the wool and then the lamp can be lit. The tray is then held by a worshipper and moved backwards and forwards or in a circular movement before the god on the shrine. As these movements are made prayers are chanted by the worshippers. Another important item on the tray is a joss-stick which you have already learned can be burnt slowly and it gives off the fragrant perfume of incense. One of the things

which this symbolises is that the prayers of the worshippers are rising to God.

At the end of the prayers the other worshippers come forward and place their hands over the flame and raise them to their faces.

One prayer which is used in the puja is the **Gayatri Mantra**;

'We meditate on the lovely light of God, Savitri,
May it stimulate our thoughts.'

Savitri is a Hindu sun god but many Hindus would regard this as yet another way of expressing an aspect of God.

Another prayer used in the puja may be:

'From the unreal lead me to the real,
From darkness lead me to light
From death lead me to immortality
May God prosper us both at the same time,
At the same time support us both
May both of us at the same time apply our strength
May our learning be illustrious
May there be no hatred between us
May all here be happy
May all be free from disease
May nobody experience misery
Om, peace, peace, peace'.

Task 2
Draw the arti tray and write about how the items on it help the Hindu worshipper with his prayers.

Task 3
Look again at the words of the last prayer:
(a) What do you think the worshipper is asking when he prays 'From darkness lead us to light'?
(b) Copy out the last five lines of the prayer. Write a paragraph to show why this is an important prayer for today. Refer to situations which exist in the world or in your own family or neighbourhood at the present time.

12
Jewish

Prayer is a very important part of Jewish life and worship, not only in the synagogue, the place of worship, but also in the home. Mr Zuck whom you see below is offering prayers in his own home at the end of the day. He is reading the

evening prayer from the Prayer Book. Many Jews will be using the same prayers in their homes at the same time. Mr Zuck says that meeting with God in prayer gives him strength for living; he also feels that prayer is his duty to God.

If you turn the photograph upside down and look carefully at the Prayer Book you will notice that the right hand page seems somewhat different from the left hand page. This is because the Prayer Book has the prayers in the Hebrew language on the right hand page and in English on the left. Mr Zuck prays in Hebrew, the sacred language of the Jews.

Before beginning his prayers for the end of the day, Mr Zuck says

'Master of the Universe,
Behold,
I forgive everyone who has injured me,
And may no one be punished
Because of his wrong to me.'

The page he is about to read looks like this:

PRAYERS BEFORE RETIRING TO REST AT NIGHT

Blessed art thou, O Lord our God, King of the universe, who makest the bands of sleep to fall upon mine eyes, and slumber upon mine eyelids. May it be thy will, O Lord my God and God of my fathers, to suffer me to lie down in peace and to let me rise up again in peace. Let not my thoughts trouble me, nor evil dreams, nor evil fancies, but let my rest be perfect before thee. O lighten mine eyes, lest I sleep the sleep of death, for it is thou who givest light to the apple of the eye. Blessed art thou, O Lord, who givest light to the whole world in thy glory.

God, faithful King.

Hear, O Israel: the Lord our God, the Lord is One.

Blessed be his name, whose glorious kingdom is for ever and ever.

And thou shalt love the Lord thy God with all thine heart, and with all thy soul, and with all thy might. And these words, which I command thee this day, shall be upon thine heart: and thou shalt teach them diligently unto thy children, and shalt talk of them when thou sittest in thine house, and when thou walkest by the way, and when thou liest down, and when thou risest up. And thou shalt bind them for a sign upon thine hand, and they shall be for frontlets between thine eyes. And thou shalt write them upon the door-posts of thy house, and upon thy gates.

And let the pleasantness of the Lord our God be upon us: and establish thou the work of our hands upon us; yea, the work of our hands establish thou it.

סדר קריאת שמע על המטה:

בָּרוּךְ אַתָּה יְיָ אֱלֹהֵינוּ מֶלֶךְ הָעוֹלָם· הַמַּפִּיל חֶבְלֵי שֵׁנָה עַל־עֵינַי וּתְנוּמָה עַל־עַפְעַפָּי· וִיהִי רָצוֹן מִלְּפָנֶיךָ יְיָ אֱלֹהַי וֵאלֹהֵי אֲבוֹתַי שֶׁתַּשְׁכִּיבֵנִי לְשָׁלוֹם וְתַעֲמִידֵנִי לְשָׁלוֹם· וְאַל יְבַהֲלוּנִי רַעְיוֹנַי וַחֲלוֹמוֹת רָעִים וְהַרְהוֹרִים רָעִים· וּתְהִי מִטָּתִי שְׁלֵמָה לְפָנֶיךָ· וְהָאֵר עֵינַי פֶּן־אִישַׁן הַמָּוֶת· כִּי אַתָּה הַמֵּאִיר לְאִישׁוֹן בַּת־עָיִן· בָּרוּךְ אַתָּה יְיָ· הַמֵּאִיר לָעוֹלָם כֻּלּוֹ בִּכְבוֹדוֹ:

אֵל מֶלֶךְ נֶאֱמָן:

שְׁמַע יִשְׂרָאֵל יְיָ אֱלֹהֵינוּ יְיָ אֶחָד:

בָּרוּךְ שֵׁם כְּבוֹד מַלְכוּתוֹ לְעוֹלָם וָעֶד:

וְאָהַבְתָּ אֵת יְיָ אֱלֹהֶיךָ בְּכָל־לְבָבְךָ וּבְכָל־ נַפְשְׁךָ וּבְכָל־מְאֹדֶךָ: וְהָיוּ הַדְּבָרִים הָאֵלֶּה אֲשֶׁר אָנֹכִי מְצַוְּךָ הַיּוֹם עַל־לְבָבֶךָ: וְשִׁנַּנְתָּם לְבָנֶיךָ וְדִבַּרְתָּ בָּם בְּשִׁבְתְּךָ בְּבֵיתֶךָ וּבְלֶכְתְּךָ בַדֶּרֶךְ וּבְשָׁכְבְּךָ וּבְקוּמֶךָ: וּקְשַׁרְתָּם לְאוֹת עַל־יָדֶךָ וְהָיוּ לְטֹטָפֹת בֵּין עֵינֶיךָ: וּכְתַבְתָּם עַל־מְזֻזוֹת בֵּיתֶךָ וּבִשְׁעָרֶיךָ:

וִיהִי נֹעַם אֲדֹנָי אֱלֹהֵינוּ עָלֵינוּ וּמַעֲשֵׂה יָדֵינוּ כּוֹנְנָה עָלֵינוּ וּמַעֲשֵׂה יָדֵינוּ כּוֹנְנֵהוּ:

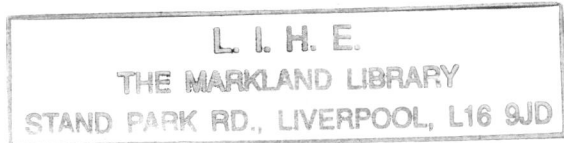

Task 1

(a) Read again the words Mr Zuck says before starting his evening prayer. Why do you think words like these make a fitting start to evening worship?

(b) Mr Zuck prays three times a day; what are the advantages and disadvantages of praying at set times each day?

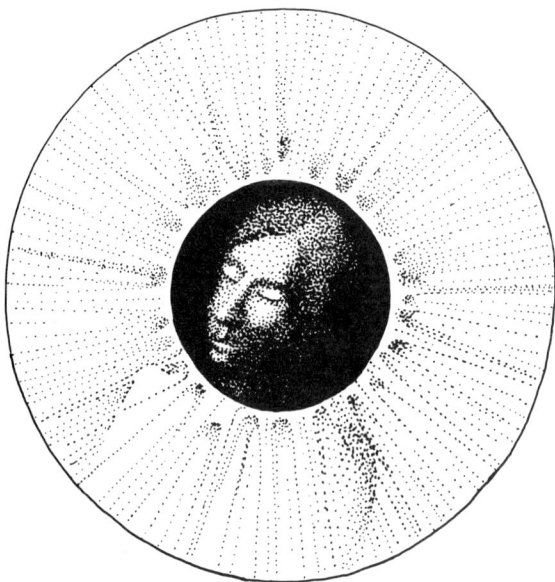

Task 2

'Who makest the bands of sleep to fall upon mine eyes'
The picture above illustrates this line from Mr Zuck's prayer: copy this picture with the words then draw some more pictures, writing below each one the line from the prayer which your picture is illustrating.

Aids to Prayer

The central statement of belief in Judaism is the **Shema**: 'Hear, O Israel, the Lord our God, the Lord is One.'

This is a simple statement from the Torah of the important Jewish belief that there is one God and he alone is to be worshipped. To remind him constantly of this belief, the Jew uses aids to prayer.

Tallith

Before worship in the synagogue or before praying at home the Jew often puts on a **tallith** or prayer shawl. The fringes on the shawl remind him of the many commandments of God which he will try to keep. He first covers his head completely with the tallith and says,

'Even as I cover myself with the tallith in this world, so may my soul deserve to be clothed with a beauteous spiritual robe in the world to come.'

He then places the shawl around his shoulders and says,

'Blessed art Thou, O Lord our God, King of the Universe, who hast sanctified us by Thy commandments and hast commanded us to enwrap ourselves in a fringed garment.'

Phylacteries

Phylacteries are little square black leather boxes which have leather straps attached so that they can be worn. One is worn on the left arm and the other is

74

worn on the forehead. Inside the boxes are passages from the scriptures, including the Shema. The phylactery on the left arm is a reminder to keep God's laws with all one's heart because it is worn near to the heart. The phylactery on the forehead reminds the Jew to concentrate on God's teachings with his full mind. Phylacteries are worn when praying at home or in the synagogue.

Task 3

(a) Draw the tallith and the phylactery and write an explanation of how they are used in worship.

(b) Find in your Bible Deuteronomy: chapter 6, verses 4–9 and chapter 11, verses 13–21: from the information there, write a paragraph on why these articles are used in worship.

Tallith and Phylactery

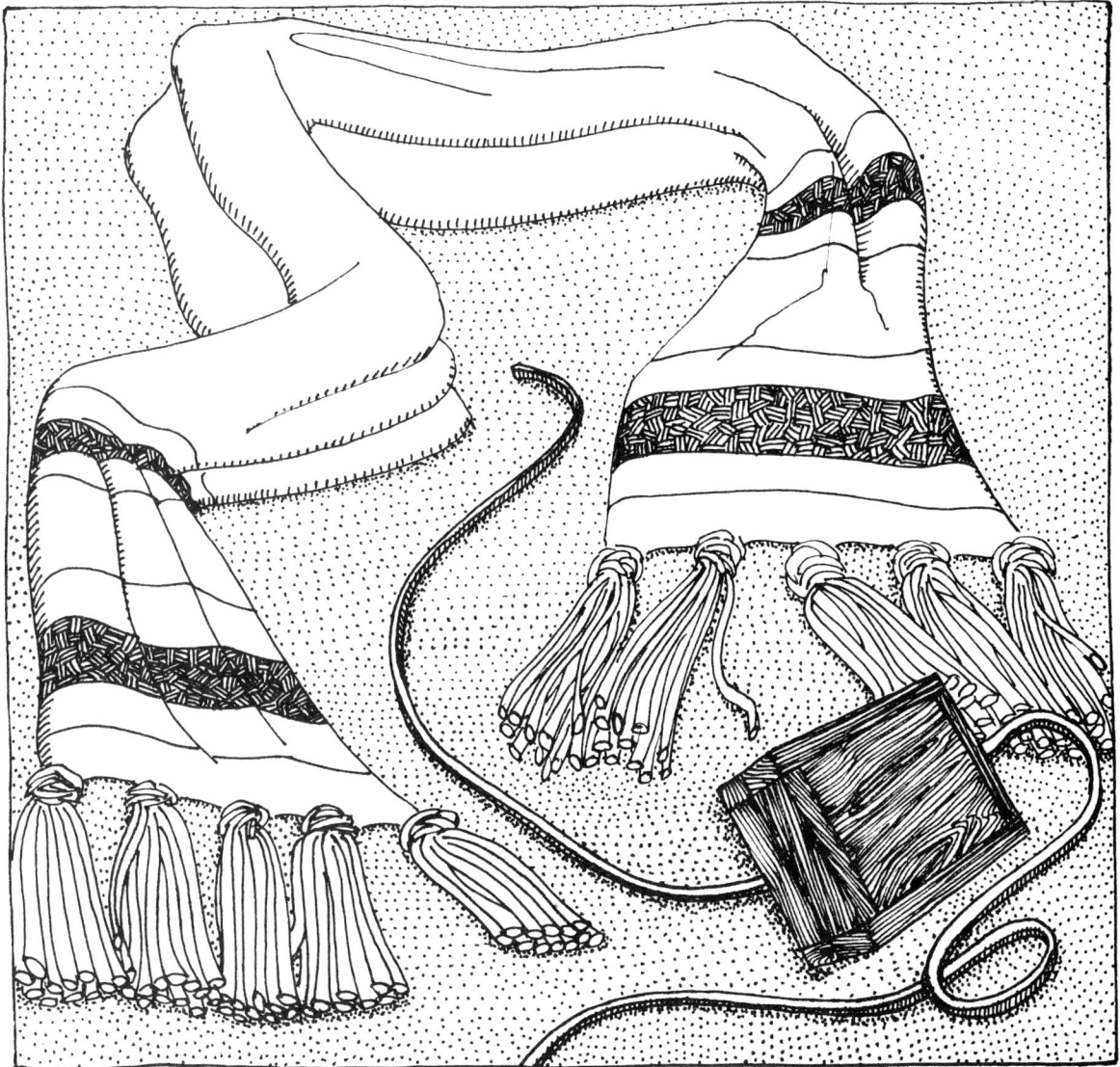

Praying on the Sabbath

The Sabbath is a very special day for the Jew. It is a day of rest and prayer. It begins on the Friday evening at sunset. While the men in the family are attending a service at the synagogue, the mother and daughter remain at home. The table is set for a meal in a special way and has on it two Sabbath candles, a special loaf of bread, and a glass of wine. As she lights the Sabbath candles, the mother may say 'Light is symbolic of the presence of God. We ask God's blessing on our family circle and we unite ourselves with the people of Israel in all lands and all ages as we kindle these Sabbath lights.'

She then prays in Hebrew,

'Baruch atah Adonai Eloheynu melech ha'olam, asher kidshanu b'mitsvotar v'tsivanu l'hadlik ner shel shabbat, Amen.'

which means
'We praise Thee O Lord our God, King of the Universe, who, having sanctified us by Thy laws, commanded us to kindle the Sabbath lights. Amen.'

When the father returns from the synagogue there is a little ceremony where.he places his hands on his

The Sabbath candles

Blessing the children

Washing the hands

Blessing the bread

children's heads and blesses them saying, 'God make you like Ephraim and Manasseh. God prosper you and make you like Rachel and Leah.'

The family prepare for the meal by washing their hands in a special way: they pour a glass of water twice over their hands saying, 'Blessed art Thou, O Lord our God, King of the Universe who hast sanctified us by Thy commandments and hast given us the command concerning the washing of hands.'

As the family gathers at the table, the father makes a blessing over the bread:

'We praise Thee, O Lord our God, King of the Universe, who brings forth food from the earth.'

The family then eats the meal together and when it is over they usually say together another prayer of thanksgiving.

Many more prayers will be said in the home and in the synagogue before the Sabbath ends at sunset on Saturday evening.

Task 4

(a) Draw four pictures to illustrate four occasions of Jewish prayer on the Sabbath.

(b) Most Jews look forward to the Sabbath and think of it as the best day in the week. What day do you think of as the best for you? In the same way as the Jew has a short prayer for anything that he does on the Sabbath, write some brief prayers which are linked with some of your activities on your favourite day.

Task 5

In the Old Testament, there is a book called the Book of Psalms which is a collection of hymns and prayers which are used in Jewish worship: the Psalm 137 is one of them.

By the waters of Babylon,
  there we sat down and wept,
    when we remembered Zion.
2 On the willows there
  we hung up our lyres.
3 For there our captors
  required of us songs,
  and our tormentors, mirth, saying,
    "Sing us one of the songs of
      Zion!"

4 How shall we sing the LORD's song
  in a foreign land?
5 If I forget you, O Jerusalem,
  let my right hand wither!
6 Let my tongue cleave to the roof of
      my mouth,
  if I do not remember you,
  if I do not set Jerusalem
    above my highest joy!

7 Remember, O LORD, against the
      E'domites
    the day of Jerusalem,
  how they said, "Rase it, rase it!
    Down to its foundations!"
8 O daughter of Babylon, you devas-
      tator!
  Happy shall he be who requites
      you
  with what you have done to us!
9 Happy shall he be who takes your
      little ones
    and dashes them against the rock!

At the time this Psalm was written the Jews were far away from their own land, living in an unfamiliar country, Babylon, and they were filled with a longing for home.

Imagine that you are far away from your own land and write a modern Psalm telling of your love of your home land and how you feel in this strange country. Remember a Psalm is usually like a prayer addressed to God so write your Psalm in that style.

13

Christian

Our Father, who art in Heaven,
Hallowed by Thy Name,
Thy Kingdom come,
Thy will be done, on earth as it is in
Heaven.
Give us this day our daily bread,
And forgive us our trespasses,
As we forgive those who trespass
against us,
And lead us not into temptation,
But deliver us from evil,
For Thine is the Kingdom, the power
and the glory,
For ever and ever.
Amen.

Almost everyone brought up in a country where Christianity is the main religion is familiar with these words. It is, of course, a prayer which Jesus, the founder of Christianity, taught his disciples, and it has become an important prayer in the Christian church.
It falls into three parts:
(a) it begins with worship to God, the Father;
(b) some requests are made to God;
(c) it ends, as it began, with thoughts about God.
When Christians pray, their prayers usually tend to follow that same pattern.
The photographs in this section are of people in different kinds of Christian churches, but they all have one thing in common – they are all at prayer.
Sometimes in Christian worship the Priest or Minister will stand in front of

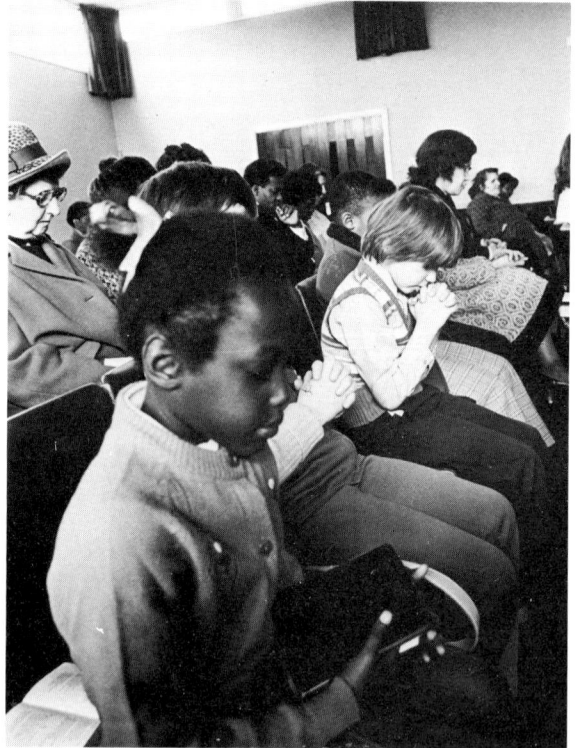

A congregation at prayer

the congregation and will lead the people in prayer.
He will usually do this by reading or saying a prayer and the people will listen and perhaps say 'Amen' at the end of it. 'Amen' means 'may it be so'.
Sometimes people offer silent prayers to God.

Silent prayer

Look carefully at all the photographs in this section on Christian prayer. Write down briefly for each one

(a) what you notice about the people who are praying: e.g. what bodily position have they adopted? What about their hands, eyes, etc?

(b) What makes you think they are worshipping rather than just being present in church?

Aids to Prayer

If you study all the photographs in this section again, you will notice that there are a number of differences, although all are of people praying. In some, the worshippers have closed their eyes, in others their eyes are open and they are looking intently at something. They may well be looking at what you see below. Think carefully about why this may help them to pray.

Meditation

Using a rosary

You will notice that some worshippers are kneeling, some are sitting, some have put their hands together, others are holding what looks like a string of beads. All these are different ways in which Christians find help to make their prayers more meaningful.

Task 2
Copy the following into your book, filling in the gaps.

Aids to Prayer
Some Christians, when they are praying believe that it helps them to concentrate if they can shut out everything around them which may distract them, so to do this they . . . . . .

Some believe that a bodily position which expresses a humble attitude towards God, helps them have such an attitude of mind as they pray, so they . . . . . . and . . . . . . or in some cases do either the one, or the other.

Others find it is an aid to their prayer if they look at something in Church which helps focus their attention on an important aspect of their faith, for example . . . . . .

Meditation
To meditate is to spend time quietly allowing your mind to dwell on some topic. Some Christians, for example, may sit and think quietly about an incident from the life of Jesus, perhaps wondering in what ways the lessons of this incident could be applied in their own lives today.

We have already mentioned aids to prayer; many Christians find meditation especially is helped by such aids. Those who are meditating may find help by gazing at some object in church, or even at a picture. Many Roman Catholic Christians use a rosary to help their meditation. A rosary is a string of beads made of wood, metal or stone.

Task 3
Read the temptations of Jesus in Luke:
Chapter 4, verses 1–13 and write a
meditation on this passage.
Begin in this way: 'Lord, when I am
tempted I remember how you faced
temptation in the wilderness . . . . . .

Different Types of Prayer

The Christian will sometimes think in
terms of four different kinds of prayer:
Adoration, Confession, Thanksgiving,
Requests.

Adoration
In prayers of this kind the worshipper
thinks of God and admits that God is so
much greater than he is himself.

> 'Worthy art Thou, our Lord and God to
> receive glory and power, for Thou didst
> create all things, and by Thy will they
> existed and were created. Great and
> wonderful are Thy deeds O Lord God the
> Almighty.'

Confession
In a prayer of this kind the worshipper
admits to his faults and asks forgiveness.

> 'O Lord, we confess how quickly we see
> other people's faults and how slow we are
> to recognise our own. Forgive us and
> make us more forgiving. Amen.'

Requests
In a prayer of this kind the worshipper
makes requests of God.

> 'O God give us,
> Clear sight
> That we may know what to do
> Courage
> To embark upon it.
> Skill,
> To find a way through all its problems.
> Perseverance,
> To bring it to its appointed end.

> Strength,
> To resist all the temptations which would
> lure
> Us aside.
> Through Jesus Christ our Lord.
> Amen.'

Thanksgiving
In a prayer of this kind the worshipper
expresses thanks to God for his many
gifts.

> 'For happy homes and loyal friends
> for all those who help us by word, deed
> and example and for all those who love
> us and whom we love, we thank thee, O
> God.'

Task 4
Look carefully at the photographs on the
previous pages in this section. Match one
of them to each of the four types of
prayer mentioned previously.
For each one write a suitable prayer of
your own. Write your prayers in the
language of today.
Set out your work as follows:
Types of Prayer
  (a) Adoration. I think the photograph
on page . . . shows a prayer of Adoration
being offered. The worshipper might have
been praying as follows . . .

14
Muslim

You have already learned that a Muslim is one who follows the faith known as Islam and that a Muslim is expected to pray five times each day. This fact in itself suggests how important prayer is to those who follow this faith. It is seen to be even more important when we realise that to the Muslim, prayer is not just a hasty sentence, over in a minute, but involves saying a number of prayers to Allah (God) and for each one, taking up a different bodily position.

The approximate prayer times for the Muslim are:

Sunrise
Mid-day
Late afternoon
Sunset
Two hours after sunset.

Men usually go to the Mosque, the Muslim place of worship to observe the prayer rite; when boys reach the age of twelve they are expected to join the men for prayers in the Mosque. Women usually stay at home, but offer the same prayers as the men.

You will remember that when a Muslim prays he always faces in the direction of the Muslim Holy city of Mecca. Mecca is where Muhammad, the founder of Islam, was born; it is in Saudi Arabia, near the eastern shore of the Red Sea. You will also remember that the direction of Mecca is marked in a Mosque by an alcove which is known as the **Mithrab**. Every worshipper faces towards that during prayers. This helps

the Muslim feel a sense of belonging to the four hundred million Muslim worshippers who, in their different parts of the world, all face towards this one place to offer their prayers.

The Call to Prayer

In a Muslim country a Mosque like the one shown here would be a familiar sight. Its tall tower is called a Minaret and from the little balcony near the top, a call to prayer is sounded out over the town to mark the beginning of each prayer time. The man whose task it is to make this call to prayer is known as the **Muezzin**.

In a Mosque in England, the Muezzin would still sound out the call to prayer. This is what the Muslim man is doing in the photograph. Notice, however, that he stands inside the Mosque and, as the worshippers are beginning to assemble, he makes the call to prayer.

This call to prayer is always made in Arabic, the language in which the Qur'an, the Muslim's Holy Book, is written.

Allahu-Akbar
Allahu-Akbar
Allahu-Akbar
Allahu-Akbar
Ash-hadu-an-la-ilaha-illallah

Ash-hadu-an-la-ilaha-illallah

Ash-hadu anna muhammadu-rasulullah

Ash-hadu anna muhammadu-rasulullah

Hayye-alas-salah
Hayye-alas-salah
Hayye-alal-falah
Hayye-alal-falah
Allahu-Akbar
Allahu-Akbar
La-ilaha-illallah

God is the greatest
God is the greatest
God is the greatest
God is the greatest
I bear witness that there is no God but Allah.
I bear witness that there is no God but Allah
I bear witness that Muhammad is the messenger of Allah
I bear witness that Muhammad is the messenger of Allah
Come to prayer
Come to prayer
Come to security
Come to security
God is the greatest
God is the greatest
There is no God but Allah

Task 1
Study carefully the photograph on page 83. Imagine you are interviewing the Muezzin in order to find out about his part in Muslim worship. Write down what questions you would ask him and what answers you think he would give. Make use of the information on the previous pages and include the words of the Call to Prayer.

The Prayer Rite

The Prayer rite is called **Salat** by Muslims. They take up a variety of bodily positions as they pray. The photographs in this section show several of these positions.

1 First of all, the worshipper raises his hands to his ears as the Muezzin is doing in the photograph on page 83. While doing this he says **'Allahu-Akbar'** which means 'God is the greatest'.

2 He then takes up the position you can see in the first photograph on page 85. He recites the first chapter of the Qur'an which is known as 'the **Fatiha**'. Before reciting it he says, 'I begin in the name of Allah, the Beneficient, the Merciful. I recite the opening chapter of the Holy Qur'an'. The Fatiha, which he then recites, is as follows:

'All praise is due to Allah, Lord of the Worlds, the Beneficient, the Merciful Owner of the Day of Judgement. Thee alone we worship; Thee alone we ask for help. Show us the straight path, the path of those whom thou hast favoured, not the path of those who earn Thine anger nor those who go astray. Amen.'

3 In the next photograph, you see the next stage of the Prayer rite where the worshipper bows. In this position he says, three times:
'Glory be to my Lord, the Greatest.'

4 This is followed by 'the Prostration', which you can see in the photograph above. This position shows that the worshipper is offering himself completely to Allah. While in this position, he repeats three times: 'Glory be to Thee, my Lord, the Highest.'

5 The worshipper then, as you can see below comes up from 'the Prostration' to a position in which he is sitting back on his feet.

After this, for a second time, the worshipper takes up the position of 'the Prostration' and repeats again the words he said previously in this position.

6 He returns to the sitting position again, as you see below. This time, he prays for forgiveness: 'O God, forgive me and have mercy on me and sustain me and guide me aright and restore me and preserve me in health and pardon me'.

He may also offer a prayer which is very similar to the Christian Lord's Prayer.

'Our Lord Allah, which art in Heaven
Hallowed be Thy Name,
Thy Kingdom is in Heaven and Earth,
As Thy mercy is in Heaven, so appoint us mercy, on earth,
And forgive us our sins and errors
Thou Lord of good things.'

7 The Prayer rite continues with the position shown below in which the worshipper first turns his head to the right, then to the left and each time says, 'Peace be to you and the mercy of God'. In this way the worshipper is taking notice of his fellow worshippers in whose company he has offered his act of worship to Allah.

8 The main Prayer rite is now ended, but before rising from his knees, the Muslim worshipper takes up the attitude you see below. In this position he offers any personal prayers he may wish to pray.

Task 2
Now that you have studied carefully the photographs which show the different positions of Muslim prayer, copy the following into your book, supplying the information required, where necessary. *Boys should do 'A', girls should do 'B' and all should then do 'C'.*

Muslims at Prayer
A.   I arrived at the Mosque for prayers at sunset; the Muezzin had just begun to send out the Call to Prayer. When we pray, we face in the direction of . . . This is marked in the Mosque by a kind of alcove which we call the . . . Also there are . . . on the floor which guide us about the distance to leave between the other worshippers in front and behind us. Usually there are no women with us at the Mosque because . . .

B.   It was about sunset; father and my brothers had already gone to the . . . for prayers. Mother and I stayed at home for our prayers because . . . When we pray, we face in the direction of . . . In the Mosque this is marked by a kind of alcove which we call the . . . At home, we have worked out the direction in which we should face.

C.   Before we begin the Prayer rite, we stand quietly for a few moments, putting ourselves in the right frame of mind for praying. A little later, we . . . (here describe the first position on page 85). While standing like this we recite quietly the . . ., which is the opening chapter of the . . . As we continue to observe the Prayer rite, we . . . (describe the second position on page 85). In this position, we say '. . .' We then come to a very important part of our prayers – the Prostration – for this, we . . . (describe the first position on page 86). We say . . . times '. . .'. We follow this with a second Prostration, again saying the words, '. . .'. For a second time, we take up the sitting position (see page 87) and this time we pray . . .; we may also pray a prayer which is similar to . . . .

Our Prayer rite nears its end with the first and second Salaam (see page 88). Here we . . . (describe the positions) and both times we say '. . .'. Before rising from our knees we . . . (describe the position you can see on this page). In this position, we offer any personal prayers. I was praying . . . (write here briefly what you think you might have prayed).

15
Sikh

Before looking at the part prayer plays in worship among the Sikhs there are certain facts which we should remember. Task 1 will help you to do this.

Task 1
Copy the following into your book filling in the gaps. Refer back to 'Places of Worship' and 'Sacred Books in Worship' if necessary.

(a) The founder of the Sikh faith was called . . .

(b) The Sikh place of worship is called . . .

(c) The Holy Book of the Sikhs is called . . .

(d) The man who reads from this Holy Book is called the . . .

Guru Nanak teaches the importance of sincerity in prayer

Guru Nanak, the founder of the Sikh faith used to say that all men are sons of one God. He could see good and bad in all the faiths which men followed. He used to get up early every morning and go to bathe in the river and offer prayers to God. On one of his journeys the local people asked him to join in their prayers. Nanak accepted the invitation saying 'I gladly accept. I am always ready to pray to God'.

They all went to the place of worship and everyone bowed and said words of prayer, everyone, that is, except Nanak; he stood silent and only watched what they were doing. After the prayers were over Nanak was asked rather angrily, 'Why did you not follow us in our prayer? You simply stood there doing nothing!' 'Ah,' said Nanak, 'I certainly wanted to join in the prayers but I found nobody here.' 'You are lying,' Nanak was told. 'Could you not see the crowd of people around you?' 'Certainly your bodies were here', replied Nanak, 'but your minds were far away, busy with all your business interests, and making money and comfortable lives for yourselves. How then could I join you?' Nanak then added, 'Words alone do not make a prayer; a prayer should come straight from your heart. I am always ready to join such a prayer.'

Task 2
(a) Copy the picture and in the 'balloon' over the head of each man, insert what you think his thoughts may have been (instead of using words you could draw a picture to illustrate his thoughts). Use the title 'Words alone do not make a prayer'.

(b) 'Words alone do not make a prayer'. What do you think does make a prayer, in addition to the words which may be used?

Sikh Prayer in a Service of Worship

Look carefully at both photographs; you can see that many worshippers have already assembled and others are just arriving. Notice how those just arriving make progress until each one in turn kneels and bows low with hands together. The worshipper may be making his own personal prayer, or he may simply be saying 'Waheguru ji ka Khalsa, Waheguru ji ka fateh'; this means 'The Sikhs belong to the wonderful Lord, may they triumph and may victory be the Lord's' or some translate it in a slightly different way, 'The Sikhs are chosen of the wonderful Lord, to the Sikhs be the victory of the wonderful Lord'.

Task 3
Study the two photographs very carefully. Look especially at the head, hands and feet of the worshippers in the queue.

(a) Describe what you have noticed.

(b) They are clearly looking at something which is special to them and which they regard as sacred. Give a description of what it is. (If necessary, refer back to the information in 'Places of Worship' and 'Sacred Books in Worship'.)

(c) Imagine you are the young boy in the photograph about to offer your prayer. You are soon going on a visit to India to see your grandparents who are still there; write a suitable prayer.

When the majority of people are ready the service proceeds, although during worship some people may still arrive,

walk to the front, bow and pray as the worshippers in the photographs have already done.

The worshippers will listen to readings from the Guru Granth Sahib; there will be singing of Sikh hymns accompanied by instruments such as those you can see below.

At the end of worship there are usually certain prayers which were written by some of the ten Gurus, the early teachers of the Sikh faith. The first is the prayer known as the **Anand**. This was composed by the third Guru, **Amar Das** who lived from 1479 to 1574. This is part of his prayer:

'O my soul, for ever abide with God, abide with God, O my soul and your sorrows will vanish.

You will be acceptable to God and he will conduct your affairs.'

This is followed by the most important prayer from the Guru Granth Sahib, which is known as the **Japji**. When the fifth Guru, Arjan compiled the Granth, he put the Japji, a prayer composed by Guru Nanak, at the beginning. It is the last part of the Japji which is regularly used in Sikh worship. The Japji contains lines like the following:

'Air, water and earth, of these are we made.
Air like the Guru's word gives breath to life . . .
Our acts, right and wrong shall come to judgement at your court.
Some shall be seated near your seat, some shall always be kept distant.'

The Sikh worshippers then listen to a verse from a hymn by Guru Arjan:

'Thou art the master, to thee I pray,
My body and soul are thy gifts to start life with
Thou art the father, thou the mother and we thy children.
We draw many blessings from thy grace. None knows thy extent:
Thou art the highest of the high . . .'

Finally, the prayer known as the **Ardas** is chanted by one man, usually the Granthi; he is the man who has been sitting behind the Holy Book and who has read from it during the service. He now comes down, stands facing the book with his back to the congregation; the whole congregation stands and he chants the words from the Ardas:

'Having first remembered God Almighty, Think of Guru Nanak
Then of Angad and Amar Das and Ram Das,
May he help us!
Remember Arjan, Hargobind and the Holy Har Rai:
Let us think of Holy Har Krishan whose sight dispels all sorrow.

The Granthi chants the Ardas

94

Let us remember Teg Behadur and the nine treasures shall come hastening into our homes.
May they all assist us everywhere.
May the tenth King, the Holy Guru Gobind Singh
The Lord of Lords and protector of the faith assist us everywhere.
Turn our thoughts, O Khalsa to the teachings of the Guru Granth Sahib and call on God.'

The whole congregation says together 'Waheguru' (wonderful Lord). The Granthi then continues the prayer which reminds the Sikhs of men and women who have kept the faith and even died for it.

The final part of the prayer is said by the whole congregation:

'By the grace of God Almighty
The body of the Khalsa was created:
All the Sikhs are hereby commanded
To look upon the Granth Sahib as the Guru;
Let him who desires to hold me
Cast his eyes upon the Guru Granth
Those who are pure in heart
Can find their guidance in its hymns
The Khalsa shall reign supreme
And none shall be kept in subjection;
Those who are oppressed shall be united,
Those who seek the Lord's protection shall be saved:
The name, Waheguru is a ship
Whose passengers safely cross the ocean.
Those who give selfless service,
Will be assisted by the Guru himself.
Our protector is he who is crowned with the plume
And whose hand bears the double-edged sword.'

Task 4

(a) List the important prayers which are recited at the end of a Sikh service of worship.

(b) Study the photographs and read again the paragraph about the prayer called Ardas. Now write a few sentences into your book, beginning as follows: 'In the photograph on page 94 it is obvious that the Ardas is being recited because . . .'

(c) Read again the first part of the Ardas and answer the following questions:

(i)   What are the nine treasures referred to in the prayer?

(ii) What is the tenth treasure?

(iii) Why do you think the Sikh considers these as treasures?

(iv) What nine treasures would you want to come hastening into your home?

Index